KNOW THYSELF

BY

NA'IM AKBAR, PH.D.

MIND

PRODUCTIONS

MIND PRODUCTIONS & ASSOCIATES
324 N. COPELAND STREET
TALLAHASSEE, FL 32304
(850)222-1764

FIRST PRINTING: FEBRUARY 1999
SECOND PRINTING: AUGUST 2000
THIRD PRINTING: MARCH 2004
FOURTH PRINTING: APRIL 2007
FIFTH PRINTING: JULY 2011
SIXTH PRINTING: FEBRUARY 2013
SEVENTH PRINTING: MAY 2015
EIGHTH PRINTING: APRIL 2017

COVER DESIGN: THOMAS RASHEED

PUBLISHED BY MIND PRODUCTIONS & ASSOCIATES, INC.
TALLAHASSEE, FLORIDA 32304
U.S.A.

LIBRARY OF CONGRESS CATALOG NUMBER: 98-068605

ISBN: 0-935257-06-3

DEDICATION

To all of those wonderful African-american
Teachers, now with the ancestors, who
Committed their lives to teaching us
Knowledge of who we are
And from whom I learned so much.

Namely, some of them are:

Mary McCleod Bethune
Melvin Arthur Butler
John henrik Clarke
Eunice S. Carter
W.E.B. DuBois
Matthew H. Estaras
Asa G. Hilliard, III
Theresa I. Lang
Delores G. McGhee
James J.Mitchell
Queen Mother Moore
The honorable Elijah Muhammad
Ivan van Sertima
Faleda L. Webber
Amos Wilson
Carter G. Woodson
Bobby Wright
Eloise J. Wright

ACKNOWLEDGEMENTS

There are always so many wonderful and powerful forces both seen and unseen that work to make a project such as this successful. It is always impossible to identify all of those forces, but we are obligated to name some of them and seek the forgiveness of those whose names we might omit. There remains a regular cadre of people around me who actively facilitate my day-to-day activities and deserve recognition as contributors to this project on many levels. This cadre is my office staff, including Dwayne Cole, a dedicated and hard worker who continues to bring such wonderful creativity to our operations; Spencer Conner, Byron Thomas and Syiddah Mu'min who handle so many things in so many ways that a job description would take volumes.

Professor Thomas Rasheed designed this wonderful cover for me and I am privileged to know a man of such considerable talent. I am grateful to him for squeezing me into a schedule that was overwhelming. With very short notice, Dr. Asa G. Hilliard III, my long time friend, colleague and fellow traveler along this road to Truth agreed to do the Foreword to this volume. He readily agreed even without seeing the manuscript, then read it and promptly shared his penetrating vision that captured the motive behind the book. Thank you, Asa, for always seeing so much and helping us to understand what we see.

Paul Beich deserves particular recognition and appreciation for the completion of this project. Paul was a former student of mine from Florida State University who has remained a friend since his graduation over a decade ago. During one of our conversations, several months ago, I shared with him my difficulty in locating a good and affordable editor for this project and he readily offered his assistance. Though this was a first time effort of this nature for him, I was confident in his skills and he did a quick and impressive job and helped to bring the project to its conclusion. It was his kindness and loyalty that motivated his tremendous contribution in helping me to refine this volume. Thank you, Paul for caring and giving so much.

I must give a "shout-out" to those people whose phone calls and kind words keep me inspired and convinced that it's all worth it and I am sane after all. Thank you, Nashid Fakridden, Jeanette Sabir-Holloway, Adib Shakir, Iyanla Vanzant, Lester Bentley, Eric Abecrumbie, Joseph McMillan, Wade Nobles, Phil McGee, Minister Farrakhan, Barbara King, Nathan McCall, Alfonso Murrill, Brent McPherson, Benson Cooke, Alvin Turner, Abdul Shakir, Susan Taylor and so many others.

As always, I acknowledge and thank the Creator. I remember those Ancestors who opened the way and those who taught me, especially those teachers to whom this work is dedicated. I am always grateful for the wonderful support of my children (Shaakira, Tareeq and Mutaqee), their generation and their children yet unborn, who inspire me to take on the work of helping us to know ourselves.

FOREWORD

"Sharpen your eye,
Tune your ear,
So you will know what you see,
Understand what you hear."
Listervelt Middleton, from **On the Origin of things.**

It is a high honor for me to have the opportunity to write this Foreword. Dr. Akbar's work over the past decades has demonstrated his intimate connection to our African family and to our culture and worldview. He speaks and writes with extreme clarity that is rooted in African deep thought. Dr. Akbar sends simple messages based on profound insight, reflecting the value of African culture as well as an understanding of hegemony, especially the ideological aspects of it. He is one of our best advocates for independence, in particular, mental independence that has propelled his struggle on our behalf.

Dr. Akbar is one of the founders of African Psychology, an approach to mental health and healing and especially mental liberation. African people have been healers for thousands of years, including mental healers. Our own cultural traditions include our response to the definition of health, including mental health. African Psychology has the dual responsibility of making our people whole, that is introducing us to us, and second(ly) of exposing our enemies and their strategies and tactics. This includes, especially the misusers of psychology as an instrument of oppression, including mental oppression of African people.

Dr. Akbar's love for African people is reflected in the fact that in all of his many works, we are his special audience, his family. Once again, he has fashioned a powerful message to us about us. It is practical. It is the fruit of our own deep thought and of our own ancestral heritage. In this book, Dr. Akbar soars with the likes of DuBois', **The Souls of Black Folk,** Ngugi Wa Thiong'o, **Decolonization of the African Mind: The Politics of Language in African Literature,** Chinweizu's **Decolonizing the African Mind,** Ben-Jochannan's **Cultural Genocide in the African Studies Curriculum, Marcus Mosiah Garvey's Life and Lessons** (Edited by Robert Hill), Stephen Bantu Biko in **Steve Biko: Black Consciousness in South Africa,** (Edited by M. Arnold), K. Kia Bunseki Fu-Kiau's **Mbongo** and many other African thinkers who see as the central problem of our time as the *throwing off of European control over the minds of African people.* Above all, Dr. Akbar uses Carter G. Woodson's **Miseducation of the Negro** as the springboard from which to address a variety of important issues in the mental liberation of African people.

Henry Berry (addressing the Virginia House of Delegates):
We have as far as possible, closed every avenue by which light

i

may enter their minds. If we could extinguish the capacity to see the light, our work would be complete. (Browder, 1996).

The central objective in decolonizing the African mind is to overthrow the authority which alien traditions exercise over the African. This demands the dismantling of white supremacist beliefs, and the structures which uphold them, in every area of African life. It must be stressed, however, that decolonization does not mean ignorance of foreign traditions, it simply means denial of their authority and withdrawal of allegiance from them. Foreign traditions are part of the harvest of human experience. Once should certainly know about them, if only because one must know one's environment, and especially one's enemy. One should certainly use items from other traditions provided they are consistent with African cultural independence and serve African objectives; but one should neither ape nor revere them, let alone sacrifice the African interest to them.(Chinweizu, 1987).

But it's most important area of domination was the mental universe of the colonized, the control through culture, of how people perceived themselves and their relationship to the world. Economic and political control can never be complete or effective without mental control. To control a people's culture is to control their tools of self-definition in relationship to others. (Chinweizu, 1987).

Mental liberation requires that we locate ourselves on the time line and map of human history, that we name and define ourselves, and that we rectify the problem of the loss of knowledge of self wherein we are "overwhelmed by other people's knowledge." Today the formal education of most people of African ancestry is usually accomplished in systems that take us far away from ourselves. We use the words, models, language, theories and values of others to think our thoughts and solve our problems. These others see us as objects. By looking through their lenses we come to see ourselves as objects as well. This is precisely what Carter Woodson has called miseducation and DuBois called "double consciousness, always looking at the world through the eyes of others." That is the worst of what he calls "double consciousness."

Dr. Akbar sees clearly the importance of African cultural experiences to the problem of liberation. It is not just that others dominate us in our thinking. The real problem is the nature of the worldview of those who seek to impose their domination upon us and the nature of the worldview from which the attempt is made to separate us from each other. There are competing views of the self between us and some others. For African people, universally, the self is experienced as social and spiritual. It is extended and collective. It emphasizes the bond to our people and the bond to our creator. The personal self is not emphasized by people of African ancestry who identify with our African cultural core. As Dr. Akbar shows, it is the "transpersonal self." Clarity on this matter is the foundation of what it will take for African people to liberate themselves. Dr. Akbar addresses the issue of autonomy and independence directly: "the ability of people of African ancestry to influence the physical and ideological environment, and the vision of what the world must become." African people must be players, not spectators, in the design of the future world. We must be a part of the community of ideas and agents of the development of vision in the process of bringing into being the world that we ought to have. Dr. Akbar recognizes the critical importance of seeing ourselves as an historical people, as a cosmic people, as a spiritual people. To do this is not to daydream but to link ourselves firmly to our history, a history from which our enemies have attempted to separate us. Dr. Akbar points the way to what we must do. We must be active critics of existing systems. He talks about "de-constructing," looking into, taking the system apart. Then, of course, we must take charge of "re-constructing" our own vision and strategies, to construct the world that we need. In doing this, we do not "isolate" and "segregate" ourselves from the world, but we unapologetically do claim and assert our autonomy and independence.

There is a delightful surprise in the appendix of the book. It is the presentation of a model of an inspiring renaming ritual. It is practical, relevant and usable. The mere act of reading this ritual excites and awakens consciousness and gives a tantalizing view of an important part of the experiences of our people as we approach the next millenium.

How wonderful it is to be taught by a free teacher, a spiritual leader, a member of our family who truly loves the family, an architect of transforming processes, a defender of African people, a beacon, a Son of Africa, a divine spirit manifesting our creative genius. Thousands upon thousands of people know Dr. Na'im Akbar as a special treasure. This book is another important gift from him to us. It is our responsibility to study these thoughts, carefully. To follow these teachings is to guarantee our liberation and to guide us toward our divine destiny.

Bibliography
Browder, A. J (1996) **Survival Strategies for Africans in America: 13 Steps to Freedom.** Washington, DC: Institute Of Karmic Guidance.

Chinweizu. (1987). **Decolonizing the African Mind.** London: Sundoor Press.

Wa Thiong. (1986). **Decolonizing the Mind: The Politics of Language in African Literature.** Portsmouth, NH: Heinemann.

Asa G. Hilliard III, Ph.D.,
Calloway Professor of Education
Georgia State University

TABLE OF CONTENTS

Introduction

Knowledge is the hallmark of civilized human life. That special attribute which distinguishes human life from all other forms of life on this planet is the unique ability to acquire knowledge. Knowledge is the capacity to know oneself, and to have the ability to communicate that knowledge to others. Other animals have the capacity to learn and to establish new behavior that is actually only habit or action without awareness. Human beings are capable of knowledge acquisition and this permits them to move above the level of habit and actually gain and transmit knowledge about themselves and the world that they live in, over generations. Other forms of life may alter their genetic code by altering their habits over sustained periods of time, but they are unable to leave a record of the rationale for developing certain patterns, mastering certain obstacles and breaking down the complexity of some aspect of the environment.

This remarkable and significant way of getting knowledge and passing it along permits human beings to master their environments and themselves unlike any other form of life. We are able to redesign much about the environment that we live in because of our knowledge of its patterns and its cycles. We are ultimately able to change ourselves and improve ourselves unlike any other form of life because of the accumulated and transmitted knowledge of who we are and how we function. The real mark of civilization is in the maintenance of certain systematic knowledge that preserves the code of how to overcome obstacles and understand problems that reoccur in the environment. We don't have to grow another layer of hair over the course of several generations, as the other mammals must do in order to survive the elements. Instead, we need only keep a mental record (an external or internal library) of how the cold was avoided when it came before. This mental record permits each generation to rise above those who came before because we are able to build on the knowledge of those who have already mastered a problem. Whereas it takes other animals literally scores of generations to alter their instincts in order to transmit the newly discovered messages, humans are transformed by the single discovery that is preserved and then transmitted forevermore. Transformation can occur for the entire human race by the one-time discovery of a bit of knowledge that makes everyone different from that point forward. The discovery of the use of fire transformed human beings from that generation forward. The same can be said about electricity, engines, flight, the causation of diseases, etc. Whereas it probably took the first birds several thousands of years to master flying and encode it in their genes, in just a couple of generations after the Wright Brothers, every human being on the planet is now capable of flying. Smallpox once wiped out entire populations, but once its cause was understood, it now has the rarity of a remote moment in history.

All civilized groups struggle to preserve their shared or collective information. There is recognition that the people's ability to survive and master the obstacles of the environment is a direct consequence of their ability to preserve their knowledge. There is also recognition that in the process of human competition for limited resources and preserving ourselves, we must ultimately seek to gain greater knowledge than our competitors. So each group, not only engages in the process of developing and sharing certain knowledge, they also engage in the concealment of knowledge which may give them enhanced effectiveness over their competitors. Human communities must acquire and preserve the secrets of life that ensure their survival. Each community must also be sensitive to the excessive appetites of some groups that requires the more modest to defend themselves by maintaining an advantage in their knowledge base.

Consciousness (literally translated to mean with knowledge or knowing with others) is the internal manifestation of knowledge. Awareness is the distinguishing quality that differentiates between human life that is functional and life that is dysfunctional. As a people's shared knowledge is the criteria for assessing their level of civilization, personal awareness is the way by which we determine individual functioning. There is no wonder that the Ancient African people taught the world (and later transmitted by the Greek and Roman students of Africa) that the ultimate instruction for human growth and transformation was: *"Man know thyself."* To be conscious was to be alive and to be human. The greater the consciousness the higher was the expression of ones humanity. Human beings in their highest points of development (e.g., Egypt or Kemit; Mayans, etc.) were most noteworthy for their devotion to the development of consciousness. These societies were distinguished by their commitment to developing images and structures that cultivated the human consciousness. Such societies were also famous for the devotion of large groups of people to the process of consciousness development for the benefit of the entire society. We are told that in the peak of Kemetic civilization there were actually more than 80,000 students who were studying the system of consciousness development at *Ipet Isut* (called by the later interpreters, The Temple of Karnak.) There is reason to believe that these ancient temples and all of their embellishment were developed for the express purpose of cultivating human consciousness. Even the pyramids and the mighty Sphinx were obviously more than pagan idols and Temples. It took great levels of skill to construct these mighty structures. The failure of contemporary efforts to duplicate these building feats suggests that these were examples of a higher form of science than current science and not just the clumsy efforts of a "primitive and pagan people," as some have claimed.

Consciousness is a valued human asset and every people seek ways to enhance their knowledge—particularly their self-knowledge. There is a mistaken notion that consciousness is a finite resource and many people engage in the hoarding of these resources under the assumption that if they don't accumulate more than others then they will be less effective as human beings. There has also

---

[1] The name Egypt is a Greek name given to the Nile Valley Civilization. The people of this Civilization identified their culture as KMT or Kemit. In this volume, we will refer to the land of the Great Nile Valley Civilization as Kemit as these great African people referred to themselves.

been the discovery by some that other human beings can be subjugated and made servile by limiting their consciousness of themselves and by imposing certain selective aspects of alien knowledge on others.

It is the recognition of the consequence of losing self-knowledge and being overwhelmed by the knowledge of another group of people that inspired Dr. Carter G. Woodson's[1] description of the process which he called *"miseducation."* Though Dr. Woodson applied the concept of "miseducation" specifically to the condition and circumstances of African-Americans, such a process can ultimately undermine the human endeavors of any people. In Dr. Woodson's case study of the African-American, he demonstrated the consequence of an entire group of people being systematically deprived of the knowledge of themselves. He described the personal and collective consequences in the behavior and conduct of people who lost their self-awareness because of a process of deliberate "miseducation."

In order to correct the process of miseducation and to heal the consequence of this plague, it is necessary to gain a basic understanding of what education *should* be. Though there is considerable educational philosophy and theories of education that have been offered by European-American educators, we cannot risk the use of those theories since they have been offered by a tradition of education which has comfortably and deliberately miseducated African-Americans and other non-European people. The objective of this discussion is to look at the process of education in a holistic way and to determine what should be the ingredients of an effective education. We shall draw upon the traditions of African education as a means of conceptualizing what this educational process should entail. We shall also include concepts from the teachings of the Honorable Elijah Muhammad and his highly successful educational program for the Nation of Islam. We should end up with a model for educational institutions which teach African-Americans, as well as some guidelines for the process of the reeducation of those African-Americans who have already been miseducated by Institutions that did not have their true education in mind.

Several years ago, I wrote a very popular little pamphlet entitled **From Miseducation to Education.**[2] It was a very brief effort to distinguish between real education and miseducation. This pamphlet drew from Dr. Woodson's concept of miseducation and suggested several ways that we could identify authentic education. The ideas in **From Miseducation to Education** caught the imagination of many hundreds of people who had never heard of Dr. Woodson's ideas, but immediately recognized some deficiencies in their own learning which gave living proof to the concept of miseducation. For over twenty years, I have begun my classes in "Black Psychology" with the reading and discussion of Dr. Woodson's book, **The Miseducation of the Negro.** I have found this concept of Dr. Woodson's to be fundamental as one begins to discuss the need for an alternative way of thinking. Though Dr. Woodson was a highly gifted scholar and graduate of the renowned Harvard University, the book is simple, clear and direct. It also served as the mission statement for his entire career of seeking to correct this severe problem of the miseducated "Negro." Amazingly, the original document by Dr. Woodson was written in 1933, but it is as current here at the end of the 20th century as it was during the first half of the century. It's a timeless piece, not because the problem is irresolvable, but because it so clearly identifies the far-reaching behavioral, social and economic consequences of this process. There are many contemporary African-American scholars who strongly agree with Dr. Woodson that the continuing problem of the African-American community is the fact that we have not secured adequate knowledge of ourselves. Since we have been miseducated, we do not operate at the simplest levels of our own self-interest.

In the Foreword of the small book, **From Miseducation to Education,** Muhammad Armiya Nu'man stated: "Miseducation is the root of the problems of the masses of the people. If the masses of the people were given correct knowledge from the very beginning, we would not be in the condition that we find ourselves in today."[3] This a very accurate statement and it is no doubt true, not only of the "masses," but of the leadership of the African-American community as well. The fact that we continue to make so many of the same mistakes over and over and operate so predictably in opposition to ourselves can best be understood by this concept of miseducation.

This book is going beyond the description of the problem, however. We analyze the concept of education and describe what should occur in the educational process. We build on the idea of the ancient sages of Kemit who declared that the foundation of all learning was "Know thyself," and was echoed in the clear admonitions of Elijah Muhammad that we must obtain "knowledge of self," in order to act and respond like intelligent people. Though we do not provide in this book a curriculum and the details for this proper education, we do offer some clear guidelines by which we can assess whether we are acquiring "real education" or "miseducation." We are hopeful that through these ideas, we can begin to do what Armiya Nu'man urged, in the Foreword of **From Miseducation to Education:** "(Let us) begin to think with our own minds, and not the mind of the manipulators, and consequently free ourselves from "miseducation."[4]

The objective of this publication and all of the work that I do is intended to help restore the ability of the African-American community in particular, and oppressed human beings in general, to once again think with our own minds.

CHAPTER 1

EDUCATION: VEHICLE FOR TRANSMISSION OF SELF-KNOWLEDGE

Each generation has the responsibility of maintaining the level of consciousness attained by the previous generations, and of advancing the community to even higher levels by the development of their own consciousness. Every civilized group of people establishes mechanisms by which this process of transmission is insured. The term that has come to be used to characterize this process is "education." The word is derived from the Latin verb: *educare* that means "to bring forth or to bring up." This meaning is obviously much broader than the currently accepted concept of education as a process of teaching or imposing some habits or ideas. Education in its inception was understood as a process of harnessing the inner potential that was yet unexpressed and bringing it "out" or "up" into consciousness. The process of equipping the human being with the consciousness (awareness) of their "true" nature was an essential task that every society provided for its offspring. They fully understood the gross limitation of reproducing their flesh in the young without reproducing their minds.

Education was both a sacred right and responsibility because without it, no one born into the world could become fully human. Our humanity is defined and distinguished by the development of knowledge and particularly self-knowledge, therefore it is critically necessary for each generation to learn who and what they are. This process is not limited to the transmission of certain skills and habits. Certainly there is much about human survival that has to do with the transmission of certain skills and the earliest learning that we experience firmly implants many of those basic skills, such as walking, speaking a language, etc. The development of such skills is the beginning of the educational process to the extent that they enhance our survival and are consistent with our human nature.

An analogy that we may use by looking at a lower animal like a dog gives us an idea of the difference between training and education. The dog that learns how to bark to scare away its enemies (predators), to defend itself by biting its attackers and to hunt and to feed itself is an *educated* dog. The dog that learns how to stand on its hind legs and wear a dress and dance to the music of its *trainer* is actually a *trained* dog. Despite how impressive the dancing dog may appear to the human observer, this dog has been *trained* away from its nature. Dogs in their natural element don't wear dresses and dance on their hind legs when a human provides appropriate music. Though the dog's behavior results in obtaining food and care from a master, it does not afford the dog the ability to care for itself. Such a dog is what Dr. Woodson described as being *miseducated* because the dog can perform at someone else's command but it cannot effectively command itself to do what is required for its life and enhancement. Though this may be the very nature of being "domesticated," such an orientation demands dependency on someone other than ones own resources in order to survive. This kind of learning serves the purpose of the trainer, but it radically handicaps the trained.

This trained dog is entertaining and as a human you may even pay money to see him walk on two legs dressed like a little human child. This is still a miseducated dog that has been trained by another species that exploits the dog's behavior for the enhancement of their own species' advancement. In fact, as the dog comes to depend more and more on performing for its master, it becomes less and less capable of performing for itself, and caring for its own survival. After many generations, dogs are unable to survive as are their undomesticated cousins, the wolves who are called "wild" by the human but from the perspective of its own reality is capable of independent survival much better than the "cute pet poodle." As we shall discuss below, people who are *trained* can only serve those *educated* people who were their trainers. Like the little performing dog, they will only be able to serve their masters and not take care of themselves.

Functions of education

Every society values education because this transmission process serves several critical functions. The first function of education is to provide **identity**. At birth, our potential to be human is not fully realized. It is critical that this potential should be respected from the beginning of life, but there must be a commitment to help the person achieve their full humanity. In order to become really human our humanity must be *educed*, brought forth or brought out. Identity is the consciousness of our true nature. The nature of most other forms of animal life is preserved in their instincts. There are fundamental qualities of being a dog, which are still present in the dog whether the dog has been miseducated or not.

2

The dog many not be able to engage in independent dog survival, but it is still a dog despite its interaction with a miseducation. Human beings also possess an intrinsic nature that is human but unless it is *educed* people can actually lose or not develop their human identity. People can be mammals and engage in many animal-like processes of primitive conduct of survival and life. To be human, however, implies consciousness or awareness of who and what we are. Only very little of our conduct can be accounted for by pre-established behaviors or instincts. Humans must know that they are human in order to engage in human conduct. No civilized groups of people leave this process to chance. From the moment of recognition that a new life is on the way, the existing humans (parents, family, village etc.) begin to structure the educational process.

Probably, the earliest step in this educational process is selecting a name. The name comes to symbolize the much broader reality of identity. It is with the name that we become identified among the human community and within the name is a full range of dimensions of our identity. The name usually identifies the family or direct teachers from whom we have come. The language of the name tells us much about our nationality, native tongue, culture, history and a wide range of things about our human social function and origin. Then, for most groups of people, the given name represents certain spiritual or mental qualities which the teachers intend to cultivate within this "potential" human. In Judeo-Christian and Islamic societies, many of the names are from the religious tradition and represent spiritual or inner qualities that the knowing or educated humans seek to develop in the newcomer. In traditional African and Native American societies as well, names are chosen from the spiritual legacy of the people and the name is intended to identify the higher human qualities which this new human being is expected to come to know about him or herself. *Samuel,* a common Judeo-Christian name which literally means, "name of God." *Abdullah,* which is a common Islamic family name, describes one who is a slave servant of Allah (God.) The feminine name *Hanifah* found in Swahili and among many Islamic Africans means one who is a "true believer in God." A common Akan name that comes out of Ghana West Africa is *Nyamekye* (masculine) or *Nanyamka* (feminine) which means "God-given. All of these names make an effort to identify the higher potential that is in the person and to identify the person with a Divine origin. If the name does no more than identify the day of ones birth or the nature of the weather it is intended to communicate the connection between the person and the world around her or him. It is intended to begin the educational process of letting the person know what their true human identity is.

This issue of identity lays the foundation for what the person will be able to do and what they must learn. Human beings must have a sense of who they are in order for them to demand their acceptance in the human community. This fundamental "self-knowledge" is the basis for recognizing oneself as uniquely human and being recognized by others as human and worthy of human respect. It is not accidental that the changing of the names of the Africans who were made into slaves was an initial step in the miseducation process. Being given the names of their masters or from the cultural traditions of their masters actually identified them in very basic ways as the property of their masters. People can only belong to themselves if their identity is an outgrowth of their history, their culture, their reality and their survival needs. To return to our analogy above, when the dog begins to respond to the name "Spot" or "Fido" or even "dog," it is no longer in control of its own fate as a dog with a tradition of its own independent of its master. Perhaps, this helps to better understand why many African Americans in their personal struggles against the *miseducational* process have changed their names to African names.[5]

The name that a person carries should carry the code for identifying the assets and history that they bring into the world. We bring assets that are from the history of our families and from the spiritual domain, as well as some special personality energies that determine how we will interact with the world and accomplish the tasks of our life. This identity that our names should encode will let us know and let the world know that we are bringing to the world some special resources to continue the advancement of the human family in our very special way. Actually, we can only be human in the highest sense if we have an identity that is our own. The process of "bringing out" (or *educing*) who we are can only be accomplished if our identity is an accurate reflection of the qualities that are within us. We are suggesting here that a considerable portion of education is not a universal or a generic process. What educates one person or one group of people does not necessarily educate another group of people. If we respect the origins of the term education, we understand it not as the transmission of a standard body of information, but the *educing* or bringing forth that which is within and the process of facilitating a proper identity is where education must begin.

Those people who established the European-American education system certainly followed these rules, for the development of their identity. The images that are associated with the development of basic skills are all reflective of themselves. The early storybooks and even fairy tales represent images of them, from Snow White to Superman. As their children are exposed to these fundamental skills they are simultaneously taught their identity. Every culture that exercises the right to educate their children teaches a concept of appropriate identity along with the necessary skills for handling the environment. The Chinese child who is taught to count learns these skills with examples or images that look Chinese or offer a connection with the Chinese identity. The Ashanti child is taught to read, dance and speak with images and models that give them a greater awareness of the Ashanti identity. All people engage in educating themselves with a foundation in their unique cultural identity.

From this point of view, we should not be too critical of the ethnocentric basis of European-American education. This educational system was never established to provide a true education for anyone but Americans of European descent who were intended to remain the holders and developers of this society. (This was

4

legally maintained in the constitution by the exclusion of others from participation in this system for at least the first half of the life of this "democracy.") The fact that they have structured a system of learning built around their identity which fosters an increased understanding of their self-knowledge should be expected if one accepts the basic idea of this discussion. Education is supposed to be ethnocentric in its foundation because it can only be effective in bringing-out the potential that is within if the educators or teachers know what is within. Of course this ethnocentricity is especially necessary in a cultural context that has not been able to embrace a kind of pluralism that offers respect for all cultures and people. So long as there is a cultural hegemony or imposition of one ethnic heritage over another, then the educational process can only be effective when it encompasses the cultural uniqueness of the learners. It is for this reason that people who have a functional knowledge of themselves and their identity will very carefully guard the education of their children to insure that they are taught those things which insure the development of their *true* identity.

Miseducation in its foundation is the cultivation of an *alien* identity. When people are taught that they are somebody who they are not, then this forms the basis of being miseducated. The same Dick and Jane images which teach the European-American child to read serve to miseducate the African-American child and may in fact actually serve to lead them away from the reading process. Even though little "Leroy," (Dick and Jane's Black playmate) may be found in the story, he is not central to the process. It is not his family and his neighborhood that the story is about, but he is present in someone else's reality that places him in the story. Though he or she may not be immediately conscious of this fact, they are not receiving a true education because they are not being taught their true identity. Miseducation actually begins at the level at which the person is taught an alien identity and nothing about their true identity. They learn to see themselves as players in someone else's story and do not learn their own story.

This does not mean that the miseducated person fails to learn. In fact, the ones who learn in spite of the miseducational process often become the willing slaves or "pets" of their teachers. The skills and ideas that they develop have limited or no utility for themselves. This serves as the basis for the assertion of Dr. Carter G. Woodson who said:

The so-called modern education, with all its defects, however does others so much more good than it does the Negro, because it has been worked out in conformity to the needs of those who have enslaved and oppressed weaker peoples. . . . No systematic effort toward change has been possible, for, taught the same economics, history, literature and religion which have established the present code of morals, the Negro's mind has been brought under the control of his oppressor. [6]

An effective education system must be rooted in the valid identity of its

5

students. It is for this reason that the strong cry for an Afrocentric education has gone up from the most gifted educators within the African-American community. There has been a predictably strong opposition to this proposal coming from European-Americans and Eurocentrically *trained* African-Americans. The opposition to this reasonable demand is evidence of their recognition of the depth of the issue that is being raised. The protest has been far in excess of the requirements of the demand but the protest has been brutal and intense. This intensity is because the protesters at some level understand that the demand is for the *mental emancipation of the slaves* by offering a valid education rather than the miseducation described by Dr. Woodson. This miseducation actually maintains the mental enslavement of people. Those who protest are unwilling to give up their slaves or their privileged slave status. Perhaps, even moreso, there is a fear that the structuring of an educational system for African-Americans that is rooted in their identity may violate the identity-based education for European-Americans. These European-Americans in positions of power and influence correctly understand that their children must be taught who they are if they will be able to continue to function effectively as custodians of the culture and recipients of the benefits of their influence over the environment. These power holders apparently fear that the demand by African-Americans for a right to educate our children consistent with their true identity will necessarily require a restructuring of how they (European-Americans) educate their children. The opposing "miseducated Negroes" fear the restoration of a form of enforced segregation. Because of our horrible experiences with segregation enforced by oppressors, we fail to appreciate the kind of voluntary separation that Catholics, Jews and many other ethnically distinct groups have selected for themselves. They do not see the benefit of our children having special learning opportunities at least until they have a functional knowledge of who they are. Once this foundation of self-knowledge has been established, then the young African-American is free to learn in whatever environment that they choose because they will have the ability to select the skills and information that will serve the purpose of their enhancement. This is no more a form of reverse racism or voluntary segregation than is the insistence by Catholics that their children should be educated in Catholic schools (particularly in the early grades.)

Until the educational system has been restructured in a truly pluralistic way respecting and integrating the identity of all potential learners then a preliminary "segregated education" may be the necessary solution. Segregation does not mean, as it did prior to *Brown vs. The Board of Education*[ii], that a group of European-Americans or their representatives structure an educational system that insures the miseducation and misdirection of African-American children. The

---

[ii] The landmark 1954 Supreme Court decision of Brown v. Board of Education outlawed dual public school systems throughout the South. Prior to this ruling, there were legally established separate school systems for African-Americans and European-Americans.

6

form of "enlightened segregation" that we are proposing means that the best thinkers in the African-American community structure a system of learning that is intended to educate rather than miseducate ourselves. This is not unlike how the wisest Rabbis developed Hebrew Schools for Jewish children, how the wisest Elders of the Mormon church structured Mormon education for Mormon children, or how the wisest Catholic priests structured Catholic education for European-Catholic children. Examples such as these from other ethnic communities show that self-affirmation does not presuppose the negation of other groups. There has not been any strong accusation against Jewish, Catholic or Mormon education as being "separatist" as has been slung at supporters of African-centered education.

Transmission of the Legacy of Competence

In addition to the cultivation of identity, education has the responsibility to transmit the **legacy of competence.** Every people have accomplished tremendous feats in the advancement of knowledge. They have made discoveries, mastered nature's secrets, broken codes of processes in nature, made observations that had never been made before them. These breakthroughs are crucial because they teach each new generation not only what has already been mastered and understood so that they begin at the top of the accumulated knowledge, but even more importantly it teaches them that they are specific recipients of this legacy of learning. When they read of the accomplishments of Newton, Shakespeare, Euclid, Joan of Arc, Galileo, Mozart, Queen Victoria or Michaelangelo, they are being invited to share in the legacy of their great predecessors. The objective is that the children of European descent come to know their potential for similar greatness. The fact that they hear the stories of the great European Conquerors such as Columbus, Livingstone, Napoleon and Alexander the Great is the transmission of a legacy of competence that they are told implicitly that they share. They are invited to seek the secrets of science, to reach for higher levels of artistic creativity and to be emboldened to explore and conquer space and the ocean depths because of their recognition that they are recipients of this mighty legacy.

The fact that the educational system of European-Americans focuses on the heroes and heroines of European culture is not accidental. These are the images that inspire the repetition of the feats of greatness that their ancestors have achieved. Again, this is not an unusual procedure in the process of effective education of a people. Whether it is an Ugandan child or a Japanese child, those charged with the role of *educing* what they really are, must show images of the ancestral contributors to their legacy. Yes, there is a universal human legacy that must be shared. However, people must first know their *particular* legacy before they can internalize the *universal* legacy. In a social order where race, class, even gender are represented as the basis for fundamental differences in people (as is certainly the case in American society) both young and older learners must learn the message of their particular legacy in order to draw from the inspiration of that legacy.

7

This is why it is correct that African-American children should learn of the genius of the great physician and multi-genius Imhotep from Ancient Kemit as well as the scientific prowess of Dr. George Washington Carver. They must know of the Nubian Architects of the Great Pyramids to the nameless African explorers (who came without conquest as their goal) and preceded Columbus to the American continent by several centuries and initiated a cultural exchange whose monuments still stand. Some critics of Afrocentric education have condemned the teaching of these facts to African-American children as being little more than a "feel-good" curriculum. However, they still intersperse their history books with long tales of Andrew Jackson, General Custer and notorious slave-owners such as George Washington, who they are taught is the "Father of their country."

This great "Father" tells no lies even when engaging in the vandalistic destruction of his father's cherry tree. So from Santa Claus in European mythology to Saint Paul in their religious literature, up to and including Edison, Pasteur and Einstein, the European-American child is presented with a "feel-good" curriculum about European-American greatness without apology.

The curriculum is not established for the exclusive purpose of helping students to "feel-good." It is quite correctly a mechanism for the transmission of the legacy of competence that every educational system must do. The young must be taught that they have a legacy of greatness and accomplishment that they are required to continue. It is the images of greatness, which resemble them which serve to inspire young people to become the great scientists, scholars and artists which continue to fearlessly explore the world and develop new ideas and concepts which advance themselves and the rest of humanity. All young people are similarly competent and capable but such competence will never be expressed until they are shown that they have a legacy of such competence. As they learn of their great legacy, they will join the great achievers from other cultures because of their understanding of the lineage that they share. The young people who are taught this lesson join the community of "great achievers" and are able to advance humanity and their people to ever-greater heights of human excellence. There are many White achievers who argue that this accomplishment is indicative of a genetically given superiority which actually makes them more competent than those Black or Brown people who do not achieve at the same level. These "white supremacy" advocates do not consider the fact that their achievement is the consequence of a self-fulfilling prophecy that results from knowing their legacy. Those who fail to achieve very much continue to accomplish little because they don't know their potential because they have only been exposed to the legacy of others. What is even more painful is that the miseducated persons that make great achievements credit the legacy of others for their accomplishments. The popular artist and entertainer Michael Jackson who wrote an autobiography several years ago that was entitled **Moonwalk** actually dedicated his autobiography to Fred Astaire, a European-American dancer who learned what he learned about dance by the study of African-American dancers. Jackson identified Astaire as being the source of his inspiration for the dance genius that he exemplifies in his artistic expression. How very sad that miseducation often leads us to negate our own genius and attribute it to our captors who have only exposed us to the elements of their legacy.

In order to transmit the legacy, we must identify whatever evidence of our particular greatness that we can find. This should not be done to the exclusion of telling about the greatness of others, which has been the approach for education by European-Americans. It is not necessary to diminish the legacy of others in order to learn of the greatness of your legacy. The diversity of the human family is not simply a matter of phenotype or physical appearance, but it is recognition that we all bring equally valuable contributions to the wide array of the human experience. There has been greatness and failure in all tribes of human beings. Overcoming failures has often been accomplished by admiring the greatness of those who have avoided certain errors. If a group of people only study their own achievements then they will engage in a kind of repetitive self-murder that makes them perpetuate the same errors without correction. However, the uncritical imitation of the greatness of other communities robs a people of the special contribution that comes from the uniqueness of their particular legacy. In order to maintain competence, it is necessary that each generation should know about its history of competence that assures them they *do* have the capability to achieve. Without this self-affirming information young people do not manifest their power for accomplishment.

Transmitting Acquired Immunities

We know now that people who have survived exposure to certain diseases are able to transmit immunity to those diseases through their genes, the mother's blood while in the womb or from the mother's milk while being breast-fed. We appreciate that our ability to survive hundreds of diseases that decimated populations before us is a consequence of this immunity that has been transmitted to us through the blood of our parents. Again, this serves as an analogy for another of the functions of education. In addition to the bringing forth of **identity** and transmitting the **legacy of competence,** education must also transmit many of the acquired immunities that have been learned by earlier generations and their exposure to a variety of intellectual and social diseases.

The principles of ethics, law and government that are taught and enforced represent some correctives for social disease. The technique of Europeans to deal with socially disruptive persons that they call "criminals" is an example of how they structure protection for their society and themselves. The procedure of incarceration and forced "penitence" in inhuman and unnatural conditions of isolation and control represents their solution for dealing with those who violate their principles of mutual respect and community living. There are other societies that cut-off the hand of the thief. There are even many societies that assume the privilege of taking the lives of people who fail to respect the lives and property of others. The decision to make war on those who interfere with your resources and authority over your life is another prerogative that is taken by some societies. The fact that people with certain "training" or that elders with certain life experiences are designated as judges in human disputes, is a consequence of immunities that are transmitted from generation to generation. Many of these social "diseases" are common to all communities of human beings and different communities deal with them in different ways.

Thieves and murderers occur in almost all societies and they clearly represent a form of social disease and must be dealt with. There are other diseases that are condoned by some societies to the detriment of particular groups of people within those societies. An example would be slavery and racism. These constitute social diseases only to the victims and there is seldom any sense of the need for remediation by those who practice these maladies. In an educational system that is supposed to provide a transmission of immunities, such societies would not be able to teach previously learned immunities to such diseases. In fact, those who carry these social infections in their cultural practices would not only exclude, but also actively oppose the transmission of such information about these diseases to their potential victims. On the other hand they would justify, even glorify or deny their atrocities in order that remediation would not be deemed necessary.

Again, Dr. Woodson observes:

Starting after the Civil War, the opponents of freedom and social justice decided to work out a program which would enslave the Negroes' mind inasmuch as the freedom of body had to be conceded. It was well understood that if by teaching of history the white man could be further assured of his superiority and the Negro could be made to feel that he had always been a failure and that the subjection of his will to some other race is necessary the freedman, then, would still be a slave.[7]

Woodson identifies this perpetuation of a form of mental enslavement and participation in ones own oppression as being the result of failure to learn the immunities that would create an opposition to an oppressor group. The educational system that teaches the "natural" superiority of the oppressor group and the natural inferiority of the oppressed will leave the oppressed persons defenseless against their own destruction. The lack of defense is a consequence of failing to acquire the immunity that would come from a correct education. In the European-American educational system, all young people are taught respect for the property of the powerful and the need to defend the holders of power against any forces that seek to threaten that power. The African-American child in such an educational system learns to hate the enemies of their European-American teachers but they learn nothing about how to deal with their own historical enemies. Native American children are taught to celebrate the brutal violence of General Custer

10

and Andrew Jackson against their people and to actually condemn their own ancestors who fought to defend their land and their people. Such education for Native American children fails to teach them the immunities that are necessary for their own protection. The same is true for African-Americans who attend public schools named for Robert E. Lee and are encouraged to wave Confederate flags in support of the powers which sought to keep their ancestors in slavery.

The proper education of the African-American should offer the transmission of acquired immunities. We should study detailed stories of the Ashanti people of Ghana who resisted their colonization and tricked the British when they sought to steal their Royal Ornaments and symbols of power. The stories of the many slaves who resisted their enslavement must be told. The victory of Cinque on the *Amistad* and the struggles of Nat Turner and Denmark Vessey must be celebrated as a means of transmitting our immunity to oppression. The escape of Frederick Douglas, the work of Harriette Tubman and the many others that gave their lives in the cause of abolition should be told to every African-American child. The challenges brought by Marcus Garvey, Elijah Muhammad, Malcolm X, Paul Robeson and the many others who defiantly resisted the perpetuation of European-American control over African-American life should be the catechism of each generation of our young people. The scholarship of W.E.B.DuBois and Carter G. Woodson who fought a relentless battle against the intellectual enslavement of African people, should be the intellectual immunization given to every young African-American scholar who will be "trained" by the European-American educational system. The fact that these scholars used the skills of their miseducation to form a lifetime commitment to the real education of their people should be known by every student as the way that "training" should be used.

This kind of natural educational immunity would protect us from continuing to produce in each generation those who by their miseducation continue to impede our progress as a race. In the 1930's Dr. Woodson suggested:

> *The large majority of the Negroes who have put on the finishing touches of our best colleges are all but worthless in the development of our people. If after leaving school they have the opportunity to give out to Negroes what traducers of the race would like to have it learn such persons may thereby earn a living at teaching or preaching what they have been taught but they never become a constructive force in the development of the race. The so-called school, then, becomes a questionable factor in the life of this despised people. . . .*
> *For the arduous task of serving a race thus handicapped, however, the Negro graduate has had little or no training at all. The people whom he has been ordered to serve have been belittled by his teachers to the extent that he can hardly find delight in undertaking what his education has led him to think is impossible.* [8]

11

Some 60 years later, we continue to produce the same kind of miseducated "Negroes" who are not immunized themselves and continue to perpetuate the infectious minds which have come from their miseducation. In the African-American community, we still have teachers who resist the idea that our children should be equipped to deal with racism by understanding it and recognizing its presence. These "misdirected" teachers and leaders in our communities delight in the kind of victim analysis that blames African-American people for their situation. They are the voices of calm who condemn anyone who asserts the need for African-Americans to claim the same kind of self-sufficiency and self-affirmation that other people claim for themselves. They become the voices who tearfully join in any memorial to the suffering of other groups but accuse African-Americans of being preoccupied with their own victimization when they attempt to understand the consequences of 400 years of slavery and oppression. These distorted voices are the ones that even accuse those who seek to immunize our people as being "reverse racists" when they identify the source of these centuries of oppression by white European-American people. In the days of Dr. Carter G. Woodson, he noted that "Negroes who think as the author (Dr. Woodson) does and dare express themselves are branded as opponents of interracial cooperation." The irony is that those who preach immunization for the oppressed are accused of being the carriers of the infection or dis-ease. Because of this strategic counter-attack against the defenders of the race as the enemies of racial harmony, many of those African-Americans in the educational system fail to carryout this essential function of transmitting the acquired immunities that are so necessary for the advancement of a people. Certainly, one would not expect most European-American teachers to identify themselves as the source of the deadly social disease of racism.

In addition to learning about the successful ways that earlier generations have dealt with the enemies of our people, this immunizing function of education instructs each new generation in the rituals of self-protection. For example, all traditional African societies had rituals to signify the passage from childhood to adulthood. These rituals were detailed and systematic and left no aspect of achieving manhood or womanhood up to chance. The rituals of instruction for initiation were immunizations against the inevitable infection that comes from the confusion of youth that are trying to make the transition to adulthood without guidance. The wisdom of Elders who were especially educated in facilitating this transformation for youth was used as the prevention against rebellion, confusion and the kind of disruption committed by youth who are trying to be adults but do not know how. In such societies, out of wedlock pregnancies, revolt against Elders and general disrespect for the social order did not occur. These societies had learned the importance of educating the youth about their roles and responsibilities as adults and doing it in the systematic fashion so that their "adultness" was properly *educed.*

Western societies have failed to develop such immunization for themselves because of their tremendous faith in individual freedom and in the idea that youth should be permitted to find their way and make their own choices. Youth rebellion is an accepted phenomenon in American society because there is no ritualized education for dealing with it. Those who have limited opportunity and minimal control over the forces and resources of the society generally suffer the greatest from this "infection," and certainly, African Americans are major victims of the dis-ease of youth miseducation. Large numbers of our youth end up in detention facilities, strung-out on drugs or dead in the struggle to manage this infection of not knowing how to become adults. Since we African-Americans have not developed our own educational system we do not develop the proper immunization against these ills. With the absence of the power to protect ourselves from the onslaught of these social diseases, and then lacking in the knowledge to immunize ourselves from them African-Americans and other miseducated groups become very vulnerable in this alien system.

Developing a Shared Vision

Another important ingredient that must emerge from education is a vision that is shared by the collective. This collective vision might be a nation, an ethnic group or a community. Essentially, it requires that a group with a common social destiny and common historical connection must see themselves as rising above any limitations and achieving the ascendancy of their group consistent with the highest aspirations of the rest of humanity. The vision must assure that all members share a commitment, first of all to their survival, and secondly to their progress. This vision lifts up the highest possible human goals for the community. This is not a communist or a socialist vision of the preeminence of the state or nation to the sacrifice of the individual. It is actually an ideal that urges the individual to achieve their highest expression as a part of a community of excellence. The vision shows the dignity and uniqueness of the individual while recognizing that no individual can rise above the collective dignity of their community. The community, on the other hand, has no higher significance than that achieved by respecting the individual contributions of its constituency.

Documents and ideals, which define the collective vision of a people, are essential for fostering this process. Every student in the U.S.A. is required to learn and understand the collective vision articulated in the preamble of the Constitution and in the Declaration of Independence. The ideal of the "freedom of the individual" is a fundamental virtue of this society. Not only is this vision of "individual freedom" soundly articulated in educational settings, but it is also enforced in the popular culture as well. This idea is consistently reinforced in the media and in nearly every aspect of the society. We are taught the great nobility of the wars that have been fought to preserve that individual freedom, both for citizens of the U.S.A. as well as for other people of the world. We celebrate the heroes and heroines who have sacrificed their lives for the preservation of such freedoms. The very structure of the culture serves as an educational device to generate the collective vision of the U.S.A. Despite the tremendous cultural heterogeneity of the U.S.A. society, the collective vision of the "Land of Opportunity" and the "Land of Individual Freedom" stand as shared ideals among those who have been educated into this image.

The African-American experience is particularly unique within the context of the United States because we have been conspicuously absent in the formulation of this vision. What's even worse, we are painfully aware of the contradictions between the vision and our treatment in this society. Though we do not debate the value of the U.S.A. Vision on the basis of its espoused values, we would have to approach the vision with a level of skepticism that perhaps most citizens of the U.S.A. would not. In addition we would have to bring a level of criticism which grows from our absence in the formulation process and how the "vision" has played itself out in the lives of our people and in the lives of people of color around the world.

The educational system for African-Americans would have to contain a vision consistent with our heritage and our experiences. One component of that vision would have to be the specific rise and empowerment of our people. We would envision more than a token presence on the landscape of someone else's vision, but we would see ourselves in a significant place of decision-making both in this nation and around the world. Our vision would be one of self-determination whereby we would be able to bargain with other communities and nations around the world for the exchange of goods and skills that would insure the survival and advancement of our people. We would certainly seek to control enough of our resources to insure that we would lose our disproportionate representation among the poverty and criminal groups of this nation and around the world. We would want to insure control of sufficient lands, industry and financial structures that would guarantee a level of effective living for any people who seek unlimited advancement.

This vision would have to be one that offered an environment of moral and spiritual refinement of the human being consistent with the highest values of African people over the ages. We would have to create an image of human peace and spiritual advancement where material prosperity would only be a means to insure effective physical life for the elevation of the spiritual life. This aspiration would have to go beyond the freedom to worship, but an acceptance of the nature of the human being as something considerably more than its material manifestation. This vision would have to build on the tremendous evidence that our survival and achievement was the consequence of higher powers of faith and surrender to certain universal laws of order that brought our victory from the oppression of these modern times. Such a set of concepts would be consistent with the evidence that the highest achievement of African people (and humanity in general) was at those times when these spiritual and moral principles were foremost in the aspirations of human beings. We must reconstruct the kind of high moral and spiritual values that stimulated the great advancement of Ancient Kemitic society and formed the prototype for all modern civilized growth. Our vision does not include joining in the world structured on the basis of our oppressors' vision, but on the basis of a vision that grows from our possibilities. In order to generate such a vision we would have to have a concept of our competence and our right to be in control of our fate. As we have noted above, our miseducation has failed to communicate the "legacy of competence" which would instill a sense of our ability to restructure the world in an image of our choosing. Our education would have to clearly show that we had constructed a world social order, and that such competence was still available to us. Our right to control our own fate is a concept that would have to grow out of an educational experience that had identified our divinely given authority to exercise the same "will" over our conduct as others have exercised over themselves (and even, over us.) Our miseducation has fully convinced us of the rights of others to make war, create God in their physical image, take the lives of millions of human beings based on the claim for land and enslaved millions of others based on a myth of racial superiority. Certainly, a civilized people would not aspire to imitate this level of human exploitation, but certainly one would want an education that equipped them to protect themselves from such barbaric destruction.

Our education must be more than a curriculum guide that covers some of the information gaps. It definitely must afford us more than equal performance on measures or standards that have been defined by other people. The education that we receive must offer us a true and valid **identity**, it must transmit a **legacy of competence**, a legacy of **acquired immunities** and ultimately, a **shared vision**. These dimensions of an educational system actually accomplish the task of *"educare"* or bringing forth those qualities that are necessary for the affirmation of the human being. The opportunity for African-Americans to be truly human and to exercise our full capacity as human beings can only occur when we have an educational philosophy and system that will transmit these qualities.

KNOW THYSELF

CHAPTER 2

THE DEFINITION OF SELF

*It is knowledge of self that the so-called Negroes lack
which keeps them from enjoying freedom, justice and
equality. This belongs to them divinely as much as it
does to other nations of the earth.*
Elijah Muhammad [9]

The major premise of effective education must be "self-knowledge." In order to achieve the goals of identity and empowerment that we have described above, the educational process must be one that educes the awareness of who we are. This is not anything that's terribly mystical or complex. It really makes intuitive sense about what education should be. When we look closely at the European-American education system with which we are already quite familiar we see that the fundamental idea behind this system is exactly this objective of self-knowledge. It is not accidental that "world history" centers on the European participation in the world. It is not accidental that a study of "world religions" looks at the world's religions from the perspective of Judeo-Christian religions as the norm. It should be no surprise that the history of America begins with the entrance of the Europeans and the concept of knowledge and civilization has its dawning with the rise of European scholarship. European scholars admit that human activity predates the European entrance on the stage of human civilization by tens of thousands of years. This only receives limited mention in the European educational system, as do all of the other scientific, artistic and philosophical discoveries that precede European participation. This exclusive focus on themselves is not due to ignorance because there is certainly no failure to acknowledge that, for example, Nile Valley (so-called "Egyptian") civilization was already old when Europeans showed up. They certainly acknowledge that China's civilization was already ancient when the Europeans found their way there and certainly America was fully occupied when the European explorers stumbled on the American continent.

There is apparently another motive behind this exclusion of the significance of other people's contributions to world civilization. Though we are not very familiar with the Chinese, Persian, Nubian or traditional Yoruba system of education, they would no doubt focus on their presence on the world's stage as the emphasis for their educational system as well. To give the European-Americans the benefit of the doubt, we can understand the bias in their educational system as being directed towards the enhancement of their self-knowledge and not necessarily directed towards the deprivation of non-Europeans from obtaining knowledge of themselves. For the sake of the argument we are developing here, it would seem that their educational system is very respectful of the fundamental criteria for providing a good education for oneself and that is, it should be directed towards the objective of obtaining self-knowledge.

When we discuss developing an educational system for African-Americans that will not result in "miseducation," we should set as our criteria the process of "self-knowledge." We must be very careful that our definition of this process is consistent with our true identity and not working with assumptions of an alien identity. The European-American concept of "self" is limited to the experiences of the individual. In fact, their concept of self is more consistent with what Western Psychologists would consider "ego" or what we will describe below as the dimension of the "personal self." This idea sees the person as restricted to the separate space and time where their body exists. As we shall see, below, this is certainly a part of the self, but it is not the totality of the self from the African perspective.

What is the African Self?

An African-American educational system rooted in self-knowledge must begin with African definitions in order to be successful in achieving its goals. The African self is a multidimensional occurrence that is represented within the individual person, but also transcends the individual; it is in the present, but also transcends time. If one could chart a two dimensional concept of the Africa view of the self, it might look something like Figure 1.

In order for us to obtain knowledge of self, one does not simply gain insight into ones individual ego and its experiences but instead, the self is considered in this holistic way that ultimately encompasses the entire cosmos. Let's look at each

African Concept of Self

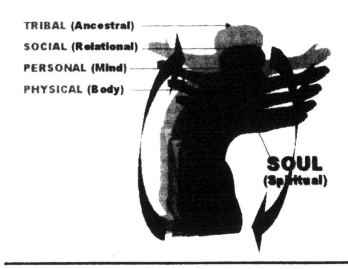

TRIBAL (Ancestral)
SOCIAL (Relational)
PERSONAL (Mind)
PHYSICAL (Body)

SOUL (Spiritual)

Figure 1: This diagram pictures the dimensions of the "self" as it is understood in traditional African thought. The person is composed of a spiritual core (soul), a physical body, a personal mind, a social self and a tribal (ancestral) self.

dimension or layer of the self from this African perspective and consider what the educational experience must be like.

The Soul as core of the Self

In an earlier publication entitled **Light from Ancient Africa**[10] I discuss the ancient African conception of the self as having the soul or *Ba* at its core. The Ancients of the Nile Valley Civilization considered the *Ba* to be the essence of the self. It represented a combination of spirit and intelligence. It is believed to be the energy that comes directly from the Creator, and it remains the human being's link with the Creator. The *Ba* is the "breath of life" which is an allegory for the universality of life that runs through all humans.

The basic educational lesson of the self is a metaphysical or spiritual study. It tells us that the essence of the human make up is a spiritual entity that has its origin in the Creator of the universe. Such an assumption would conflict with most Western ideas of the human personality because whether communist or capitalist there is considerable skepticism about the reality or relevance of a Creator. The danger of mixing up secular and sacred issues creates immediate confusion for the non-African thinker. In fact the very implication of a "religious" concept like soul would render this discussion of the self unacceptable in

19

many arenas of European-American scientific settings. On the other hand, one would be completely inauthentic within the African context if you did not consider the Divine origins of the self. Without this foundation in the spiritual domain, ones discussion would be completely inauthentic as an African system.

The soul is not a "religious" concept when Africans speak of the self. It is a scientific entity which is as evident as is light when you say "sun" or wet when you say "water." Different scientists may have varying theories about the composition and origins of light and wetness, but only a fool would deny their self-evident presence. So it is with the soul when one thinks of the self from the African perspective. This tells us that we are not simply animal creatures but are endowed with special genius, not only in our physical capability but also in our mental and moral capacity. This African approach tells us that in order to appreciate the core of what we are, we must begin by understanding the universe as a Divine Creation and to see ourselves as a part of a Divine drama. This approach looks at the human being from the inside out rather than the Western approach that studies the human being from the outside in or just on the basis of what is manifested on the outside or the observable parts of the human being. Western "objective" science only describes the outer expression of things and though it may describe these processes well, it can never answer the questions of why and where human life is going until it understands the invisible plan. This is why the science of the African world has always been a religious science, not for the purpose of creating a dogma but in pursuit of knowledge about spiritual and moral laws rather than just the metaphor of their expression in the physical domain.

This idea that the core of the self is the soul requires that education must address this spiritual and moral essence of the human being. The idea of the sacred and the secular being separate worlds that should stay away from each other would never make sense in the African understanding of education. The debate regarding the separation of church and state in the Western educational system could only occur in a worldview that accept the core of the human being as being something other than spiritual. When the concept of spirituality is reduced to dogma (church, synagogue or mosque doctrine) then the issue of separation of church and state is a necessary debate. In the way of the African world, spirituality is a given and does not get confused with religious doctrine, therefore the necessity to understand the spiritual nature is a part of the educational process. Not only is the understanding of oneself as a spiritual creature a part of the educational process but the understanding of the spiritual nature of the world is a part of the educational process. From the western point of view, the interpretation of the self or the natural world from a spiritual point of view is either viewed as being within the domain of religion at the best or just superstition or bad science at the worst. When African scientists such as the traditional healers or the scientists of Ancient Kemit are studied, they are dismissed as either being superstitious or confused about the *true* ways of science. This condemnation of African science is done despite the evidence of superior accomplishment in the construction and techniques of African scientists. For example, the repeated efforts to duplicate the construction of the pyramids using Western principles of science have not proven successful. Efforts to explain forms of healing which come from African traditional medicine are increasingly being co-opted, but still not acknowledged as having a basis unavailable to Western Science. This difference in Western and African science has been discussed in two of my earlier publications: **Natural Psychology and Human Transformation**[11] and **Light From Ancient Africa**.[12]

An educational system based in the self-knowledge of African people must help the student to understand themselves as spiritual creatures with a

Figure 2: An illustration of the Kemetic goddess, Maat.

Divinely given Will which will help them to master their physical and mental selves. They must understand the creativity that has been given to them and their power to conceive, believe and make things be. They must understand the power of the mind as a Divine gift that is not just an instrument for data processing, but a center for the Divine presence within the human being. This means that we are only partially locked into the limitations of time and space, because the soul is our timeless nature that actually transcends our physical manifestation. An educational system must be moral in the sense that the person learns truth, order, righteousness, harmony or the principles of *Maat*. *Maat* is the symbol for the principle of Truth and Balance that rules in the universe. It was depicted as a goddess in Ancient Kemit, but this image was only a physical illustration of a higher principle that rules in the cosmos.

The educational system of Africa focussed on moral instruction as the essential part of learning. The translation of works such as **The Husia**[13] by Dr. Maulana Karenga and **The Teachings of Ptahhotep: The Oldest Book in the World**[14] edited by Dr. Asa Hilliard are examples of the importance of such moral instruction as a part of one of the world's most successful educational systems, that of Ancient Kemit. The continuation of such moral instruction in the proverbial teachings of West African societies demonstrates the persistence of this idea that the soul must be cultivated as an important component of the educational system.

KNOW THYSELF

An example of the teachings from **Ptahhotep**
   Principle #8:
   If you are a man who leads, a man who controls the affairs of many,
   then seek the most perfect way of performing your responsibility
   so that your conduct will be blameless. Great is Maat (truth,
   justice and righteousness). It is everlasting. Maat has been
   unchanged since the time of Osiris. To create obstacles to the
   following of laws, is to open way to a condition of violence.
   The transgressor of laws is punished, although the greedy person
   overlooks this. Baseness may obtain riches, yet crime never
   lands its wares on the shore. In the end only Maat lasts. Man says,
   "Maat is my father's ground." [15]

The above example is an indication of how morality is an integral part of the educational system as the Ancients of the Nile Valley Civilization conceived it. Another example from the **Book of Kheti** as quoted by Maulana Karenga in the **Husia** shows another example of the role of morality in the Nile Valley's concept of education:

   Speak truth in your house that the princes of the earth may respect
   you. Righteousness is fitting for a ruler. For it is the front of the
   house that inspires respect in the back. Do that which is right that
   you may live long upon the earth. Comfort the weeper and oppress
   not the widow. Drive no one away from the property of his or her
   father. Defraud not the nobles of their property. Beware of punishing
   unjustly. Do not kill for it will not profit you... [16]

These principles were the fundamental ideas of ancient education. They addressed the spiritual core of the individual's make-up and were assumed to be the essence of education. These moral instructions were intended to educe the spiritual core or soul of the African self. This tradition of education by moral instruction has been continued into African proverbs that emphasize morality as an essential part of learning.

In West Africa, the following proverbs reflect the value of these thoughts:

   "A wise man who knows his proverbs can reconcile difficulties."
   "A proverb is the horse of conversation: when the conversation
   lag,. a proverb revives it."
   "What the child says, he has heard at home."
   "If you offend, ask for pardon; if offended, forgive."
   "A good deed is something one returns."
   "Knowledge is like a garden: if it is not cultivated, it cannot
   be harvested." [17]

Of course, the reader might say that similar moral teachings are found in most religious teachings such as the **Holy Bible** or **Holy Qur'an.** They would be quite correct since those teachings were evolved from the Nile Valley's educational concepts. The difference is that the moral proverbs that we have illustrated above are from the African educational system and are not limited to the religious literature. The African conception of a holistic self required that moral instruction should be at the core of the educational process. Dr. Karenga says in the **Husia:**

" . . . *given the inseparable link in ancient Egypt and other parts of Africa between the sacred and secular, the attempt to separate them makes little sense and meets with even less success. Thus the sages teach their children and the people to think Maat, speak Maat, and do Maat in secular and sacred situations. For this will not only insure a mutually beneficial community based on Maat, but also everlasting life."* (p.40)

The separation between sacred and secular instruction came about when the self was split into the sacred (soul) and rational (mind). This split continues to haunt Western education and Western psychology.

In addition to the moral teachings that emerge from the concept of the soul as the core of the self, the self-concept that is taught takes on a different form. In African education, the student seeks to understand his or her spiritual mission in life rather than just a vocation. A person sees his or her life as a divinely given responsibility that must be discovered. The study of literature and great people in the tradition of ones culture helps the person to formulate and identify what their mission may be. Fame is not the criteria for this mission, but a recognition that everyone has such a mission regardless of whether they become famous and well-known or not. Every person learns within the context of their education that they were born to execute some type of mission towards the advancement of humankind and each person must seek to identify what their mission might be. This is learned from the respect that is given to each child in the educational system as well as the respect that they are taught to show to the elders. They are learning not just manners, but the recognition of this Divine mission which we all have and which we must come to recognize. Respect for the young by the adults and the respect for the adults by the young is not simply a matter of "proper conduct," it is an outgrowth of the recognition of a spiritual core or essence in all of us. The manifestation of that spiritual core is primarily in the service that renders to the community that you are born into. Ones mission is to give service to others and the particular of those services is ones special mission. In **The Book of Ani** quoted in the **Husia** by Maulana Karenga, we find the following educational admonition:

23

(IX)Do not sit when one who is older than you is standing,
even if you have achieved a higher status in your profession.
No fault is found with good character but an evil character
is always blamed[18.]

The issues of *respect* and *character* run throughout the educational concepts of traditional African thought, because it is through respect and the building of character that we are able to bring forth the "soul" or spiritual essence which makes up the core of the self. Being righteous at the core and fundamentally submissive to the Divine order characterizes the ultimate nature of the human being. Because we are human and because there are other dimensions of the self, we can deviate from this core, but the core defines the true nature of our make-up. If our conduct is consistent with our true nature then we are naturally directed towards our divinely prescribed mission in life. The African concept of education emphasized moral and character development because this was the pathway through which our ancestors were able to manifest their core or soul. In understanding this fundamental moral nature, we were less likely to be distracted by the forces that come from the other dimensions of our self and our environment.

Another element of the learning of respect is contained in the idea of self-esteem. The person who learns to love their self also develops respect for the Divine core that is within. People who do not develop respect for that inner core actually can never develop human dignity. Human dignity is the foundation of conscience or what the **Holy Qur'an** refers to as the "self-accusing spirit." Children who are loved and in turn taught to love themselves develop this fundamental dignity and respect for who they are. This is why the primary lesson of education is *love*. An African proverb says: "Children are the reward of life."[19] The teachers must love children and we know that the first teachers are parents. Children must also be loved by anyone who takes on the responsibility of education. People who never discover their mission and fail to develop moral lives are the same people who never learned to love their own souls or spiritual core. The nature of that core is known through love.

As we shall discuss below when we describe the self as a "social" entity, a part of our self-respect and dignity is acquired through the input of ideas from our environments. We have to be exposed to images that mirror ourselves which are worthy of dignity and worthy of respect. The African child who never sees African people who are respectable and dignified has difficulty learning to respect the part of themselves that they recognize as being like Africans. If the only human images that are presented to them in their education are images of dignified people who are not Africans, then they have difficulty finding mirrors of themselves in their education. The identification with alien models is a fundamental part of the miseducation process. So even though they may have been loved in the home and even in some of their classrooms, there will be a defect in their self love if they do not find confirmation for that love and respect in their

24

social environment. The power of love in the home and even in isolated parts of the social environment is often effective enough to cultivate self-love even when much of the environment fails to affirm oneself. This is why so many effective and impressive African-Americans came out of the "Old South" and Northern Ghettos, where the predominant influence gave a negative image of African-Americans. *A little bit of love goes a long way!*

An essential part of education is to see oneself (as a social or tribal being) shown in respectable and dignified contexts. Again, there is no shortage of this quality when we analyze the educational system of European-American people. These qualities that I am suggesting being necessary for the proper education of African-American children are neither radical nor unknown. They are actually quite common elements in the educational system that European-Americans have set up for themselves. There are strong messages of self-love and self-respect that run throughout those systems. It is simply that the qualities of "self-love" in that system do not serve the educational needs of African Americans. What is considered "radical," is the recognition that African-Americans need an educational system that is reaffirming of them as the European-American system reaffirms its people.

The Personal Self:

This dimension of the self represents that layer of individual personal experiences that have occurred in ones lifetime. If we understand our souls as the universal core of life that is the essence of our being, entering into our particular life experience and life space, then the experiences of this lifetime represent our unique and special journey. So, the learning, pains, joys, habits that we develop along our personal journey become the content of the *personal self.* Education cannot provide specific instruction about these unique experiences but it should equip the person to better understand the experiences they have had. They should learn how habits are formed, how hurts persist, how rewards have shaped us, how role models have influenced us, how the media has structured our beliefs. This level of education comes through introspection and the tools for introspection, each student must learn. The process of looking inside of ourselves and remembering the experiences we have had and how those experiences have helped to make us the people that we are is an important part of the self-knowledge process. People need to understand how economic hard times and affluence can affect people in very different ways. The influence of political, religious and social environments on our experiences is an important part of this educational component. The autobiographical tool as an on-going curriculum for understanding who we are is an important component of this aspect of education. Writing autobiographies teaches us to introspect and to see ourselves as a developing story. We must learn to tell our story beginning at the very personal level of experience. This is another of those instances where the home should be an important part of teaching about the personal self. As we go through the family album of our baby pictures and hear stories about our development, we are able to gain an important idea of who we are as unique and separate persons.

Education of the personal self is actually what most of traditional social science is all about. When we are exposed to the ideas of the psychologists, sociologists, economists, political scientists and related fields of study, these are generally tools for understanding this dimension of the personal self. The fact that our personal history has been shaped by certain kinds of factors, we have developed certain kinds of habits and certain attitudes, which are a result of some very unique influences. Self-knowledge, in part, has to do with understanding the impact of these influences. The educational system that we are describing here sees these influences as only a component of who we are and not the whole picture. The soul as I have discussed above and the other components of the self as I will discuss below must be all considered in this process of gaining self-knowledge. Miseducation results when people see themselves as *only* a consequence of these social and interpersonal influences. One component of being miseducated is the consequence of seeing oneself as only an economic animal or the victim of a certain socio-economic environment or even as just the consequence of a set of habits and childhood experiences. This is one of the limitations of the European-American concept of the "self" that has managed to narrow the self into these small and separated compartments.

Self-knowledge requires us to inspect these components of ourselves and appreciate the role they have played in structuring the path that we are travelling. We must still remember our soul's journey and that we are ultimately only a cell in a much broader tribal self. Our cell is unique and special and it will determine how we interact with the larger world, but our self is more than just a cell. One of the cautions to prevent "miseducation" is to be familiar with the *personal* self and to know some of the qualities that are unique and peculiar to us as individuals but we must understand those qualities as only a part of a bigger self.

In addition to the personal history and experiences that have helped to shape our *personal self,* we must also seek to fully understand what are the special talents and characteristics that we have contained in our separate make-up. We need to explore and discover those special gifts that give us our unique tools for accomplishing our larger goals. There are gifts of physical strength, artistic talents, and intellectual capabilities that all represent qualities of our personal self that are important to understand. Another quality of miseducation is the consequence of rejecting certain aspects of our personal self because we have been taught that those characteristics are unacceptable. Many people fail to develop their gifts for social interaction because they have been miseducated to believe that they are "ugly," too fat, too skinny, too tall, too short. In the case of African Americans, there is the oppressive miseducation that makes us reject our talents and our selves because we don't look or act Caucasian enough. We then begin to feel that we are "too dark," or we have "bad hair" or our nose is "too large" or our lips "too thick." In the process of our miseducation, we have learned that the proper aesthetic (or standard of beauty) is the European Caucasian aesthetic and anything else is deficient. Something as simple as the appearance of the toys we play with or the characters in the storybooks begin to teach us this aesthetic. For African children, Barbie dolls, GI Joe and fairy tales should look like them. "Snow White" would preferably become "Chocolate Brown" or "Honey Tan" for our children. We should encourage our children to play at nurturing by cuddling little doll babies that look like them. Rocket scientists on video games should represent them as well as other members of the human family, but they need to see significant characters of good and genius that look like them. These barriers to our self-acceptance result in us rejecting ourselves in ways that prevent us from appreciating the unique and special gifts that we all have in our personal self. An effective education should serve to make us feel good about ourselves. To imply that we are better than other human beings just because of certain qualities in our personal or tribal selves is unrealistic and ultimately destructive to ourselves and to others. In developing an educational system for the self-knowledge of African-Americans, we would not want to replicate such a system of white supremacy that has taught Caucasian people that they are superior because they are not Black, Brown or Red people. This creates an uncritical attitude towards oneself that permits them to comfortably oppress or exploit other people without question or even awareness.

People need as many different experiences for self-exploration as they can have. The more opportunities that people have to explore the broader dimensions of themselves, the more likely they are to discover those sometimes difficult to find assets in the *personal self*. Of course, there are personal weaknesses that exist in the *personal self* as well. This process of self-exploration not only permits you to discover those hidden gems in yourself, which are special to you, but it helps you to identify those things which you do not do very well. Some people are simply "born singers," others couldn't carry a tune in a bucket. Everybody doesn't have to sing and you can waste a lot of time trying to make it in the music business without realizing your limitations in this regard. There are many young people whose parents are successful physicians, but they may have neither aptitude nor interest in medicine and may have unexplored talents in the arts that they do not explore because they have accepted self-definitions that other people have given to them. We can waste almost an entire lifetime, trying to be something that we really do not have the skills to be. A truly effective educational system will encourage an openness to explore a wide area of interests.

All men are not alike and all women or not alike. There is such a wide range of ways to express ones masculinity and femininity. A good educational system realizes that the true power of ones manhood and womanhood is the unique and special way that we learn to express it. How it's expressed is a consequence of what we learn about our personal style or way. When we are miseducated, we can spend our entire life journey trying to live up to someone else's form for expressing their gender energy. The degree to which we are rough, gentle, passionate, humorous, serene, solitary or sociable are rhythms dictated by our *personal self.* We must learn to recognize, appreciate and be comfortable with who we are, regardless of the demands that come from others. There is much miseducational information that is in the media and in the sexist educational system that presumes the superiority of one gender over the other. It is significant that most African cultures have instruction that is specialized for young men and women to explore and discover their way to express their masculinity or femininity. This instruction is offered in an environment of implicit respect for gender difference and with the fundamental assumption of the dignity of each gender. There is no need in such a system to feel limited in your personal characteristics or capabilities because you are one gender or the other. Gender difference is just another quality of the *personal self* that permits us to plot a course along the path of our life's journey.

So the *personal self* is the unique way that we express our spiritual journey. The fuel that feeds the engine in a Volkswagen is the same fuel that feeds the engine in a Cadillac. The objective is to progress along the highway of life. There are a variety of lanes, and people move at varying speeds. The type of vehicle and the speed is not the important thing ultimately, but the progress that one makes along the highway within the period that the soul occupies this dimension of time. We know that many Volkswagens complete their journeys while some Cadillacs have flat tires, burned out engines or tickets along the side of the road. Your personal self is the vehicle within which you travel and all "cars" will go! The task we each face is to find our "car." Miseducation has us looking for someone else's car and a real education helps us to find our own.

The Tribal Self:
This dimension of the self is transpersonal. When something is transpersonal it is a part of the individual make-up but it transcends or reaches beyond the individual and connects with the "self "of others. The *tribal self* is the level of consciousness that is shared by everyone who is a part of a particular "tribal" experience. The "Tribe" identifies the collective historical and shared experiences that have shaped us in the particular form that we are. A community that shares a common set of significant human experiences over a period of time constitutes a tribe. History, climate, cultural practices, life challenges and survival strategies have helped to make certain groups psychologically connected. These ties may begin as geographic boundaries that lock people into a set of common environmental experiences but eventually they can be dispersed and continue to share a similar set of characteristics.

The *Tribal* dimension of the self is the ancestral component of ones being. This is the representation of those who have preceded us, within our personality. Most communities are very respectful of this dimension of the self and show particular reverence through rituals and practices that acknowledge the continued spiritual presence of those people who have lived and contributed to our being but are no longer on the physical plane. Foreign observers have described such practices as being forms of "ancestral worship" and have dismissed them as superstitious and idolatrous. I am certain that such ancestral recognition is observed among most people on the earth. Certainly, throughout Africa one finds some form of ancestral recognition, as is the case in most of Asia and most parts of the world, except for Europe. I would submit that the prevalence of this practice is an expression of the realization of the transcendent presence of ones ancestors within the self. It is this common ancestral heritage that ties the tribe together in much the same way that the family is tied together through its shared parentage.

Consistent with the European-American focus on the physical and material as the essence of what is real, the way that is most acceptable for their discussion of the *tribal ancestral self* is in their acknowledgement of genes and biological inheritance as the vehicle by which the ancestors make their presence known in our self. The European difficulty in incorporating spiritual (non-physical) reality into their worldview, forces them to identify this transpersonal dimension of the self into a physical code that they find hidden in the DNA. Africans and most people of the world are just as certain of the legacy of those who have gone before us as continuing contributors to our being through the spiritual participation of the ancestors in our collective self. The African view of the Self places the legacy of our ancestors as an active part of the collective and individual personality.

Rituals of remembrance constantly remind the African person of the resources that exist within this component of their being. Remembering is the educational objective of this component of the self. The highly structured rituals among Africans, Native Americans, and Asians are actually educational practices. I know that these rituals are usually thought of as "religious" practices, but as we redefine our concept of the self, we are compelled to rethink our concept of education. Therefore, a part of what must be done in the educational process is to incorporate techniques that advance the awareness of the invisible or transpersonal components of the Self. One of these educational practices is Ritual. Ritual is a method of systematically reminding us of invisible presence by visible and tangible practices. This can be done by offering information that serves as a reminder of those components of the Self, but it can also be done by developing practices that help the collective community remember.

Since our focus in this discussion is on the shared experiences of people of African descent in the context of the United States, then the example of this group is an appropriate illustration of this dimension of the self. People of the African continent, particularly of Sub-Saharan Africa have been under an almost continuous siege for the last several hundred years. Foreign invaders from Europe colonized the African continent, took their natural resources, exploited the people, ridiculed and interrupted their indigenous cultural practices. The continuity with their particular cultural and ancestral lineage was painfully violated by a variety of political, military, economic, even religious and ideological strategies. This invasion constituted a psychological trauma, particularly when paired with the torturous oppression of slavery, white supremacy and death. Throughout the African continent, the processes of colonialism disrupted the authentic African experience and continuity. It alienated and disconnected people from their ancestors and obscured their memory and recognition of their *tribal ancestral self.*

The absence of information to help us remember this part of the self and the loss of rituals to help us recall have contributed to our miseducation and our psychological trauma. The result is a form of cultural disorientation and self-alienation that has produced an unnatural rejection of indigenous life practices and an equally unnatural imitation of alien invaders. The consequence is the tremendous difficulty that modern inhabitants of Africa have in the conduct of their affairs of government and culture. The corruption and self-destructive patterns that characterize the conduct of African affairs is a consequence of this tribal dimension of our self. This does not deny the relevance of the kind of political and economic exploitation that continues to be executed by invaders. The cooperation of Africans with their own exploitation is a consequence of this tribal mentality of self-rejection that has been learned from these centuries of human exploitation by non-African opportunists. Similar self-destructive behaviors are also common within the African-American community. The difficulty in working cooperatively and remaining focused on common objectives that would be helpful for our collective tribe or community is a symptom of the disconnection with the *tribal self.*

One of the greatest challenges of correcting the miseducational process is to provide adequate information so that one is able to learn the characteristics and content of ones tribal self. This is where the study of history takes on very direct and very important psychological implications as a tool to enlighten the self. Such a process is taken for granted in situations where people control and structure their own educational system consistent with their own self-interest. The proposal that active and deliberate inclusion of the perspective, cultural and historical experiences of formerly excluded peoples raises the anger and eyebrows of people who have come to take their exclusive educational approach for granted. Much of the protest about "African-centered" (or "Afrocentric") education has come from people who are very comfortable with an educational system that teaches the content of the tribal self of Europeans exclusively. Critics of Afrocentricity such as journalist George Will (Newsweek, February 19, 1996) argues:

> *"Afrocentrism is an attempt to 'empower' African-Americans with a 'transforming' myth. But the myth is self-inflicted intellectual segregation, and the entire project is condescending to African-Americans: tell them inspiriting stories, just as parents tell moralizing fairy tales to children."*

Mr. Will doesn't mention the myths of Columbus' "discovery" of an occupied land or the white invasion and occupation of a Black land which they renamed as "Egypt." Are such inaccurate myths "condescending" to children of European descent? What about the mythology of "Tarzan and the Dark Continent" which becomes interchangeable with fact when it comes to the exploitation and paternalistic intrusion into the culture of Africa. It seems that mythology that is "inspiriting" or "transformative" for European-Americans is acceptable, but factual information presented from the perspective of African people and African scholarship is "self-inflicted intellectual segregation" or "it's condescending to Africans" to hear of instances of their greatness.

As both sides of the argument maintain (probably quite accurately) the racial composition of the ancient world is probably ultimately irrelevant. What is relevant and necessary is the careful sharing of information that Caucasian Europeans have no more a monopoly on human progress and scientific development than do Black Africans who obviously pioneered and contributed significant human progress before Europeans had emerged from the period of their pre-technological development. In ancient and contemporary times, people of various races and tribes have contributed to the advancement of humanity on this planet. It is the simple inclusion of this fact, so that children of various tribes who currently exist in a European dominated society can be included in the collective human experience and not accept the exclusive praise of the European tribe as the developers of the planet. It is this inclusion that gives the African-American tribe information that permits them to restore contact with their *tribal ancestral self.*

Black scholars from the time of Carter G. Woodson and including contemporary scholars such as Molefi Asante, Yosef ben Jochannan , Asa Hilliard, John Henrik Clarke, Ivan Van Sertima, and others have simply argued for the need of African people to be included in the history of civilization. We cannot expect African-Americans to operate at full efficiency so long as their educational experience teaches the tribal history of their historical oppressors and systematically excludes their contributions as if nothing of value ever came out of Africa and from Black hands. The irony is that this unnecessary fear that Africans will write Europeans out of history as the Europeans have done to Africans simply reflects their recognition of the importance of "tribal history" as the mechanism by which a people will know themselves. With no evidence beyond the projection of their own conduct, European critics assume that Africans will systematically distort history not only for the corrective telling of their own story, but will necessarily exclude the contributions of others. Could it be that the Europeans fear that their children will be reduced to servants if they are deprived of good information and "inspiration" about their tribe as has been the case for the children of Africans deprived of knowledge of their African *tribal self?* As is evident from the educational system of other peoples around the globe, knowledge of ones particular tribal self does not preclude knowledge of other tribes, nor does it require other tribes to cease to study their own story.

31

As I have discussed above, information is only one form of instruction that restores the awareness of the tribal self. The other educational technique that must be explored is Ritual. Ritual incorporates pageantry, costumes, music, dance, ceremony and repetition. The information that is transmitted is on an emotional and spiritual plane and not in the tangible and concrete way that people are told about their heritage. They are able to "remember" the *tribal ancestral* part of the self by feeling as the ancestors felt and knowing their experience by the ritualistic or symbolic re-living of some aspect of their experience. For example to dance certain African dances that ancestors might have danced stimulates the collective memory in ways that words and description could never do. Singing certain songs and responding to traditional rhythms helps to revive portions of the experience that ancestors had who sang those same songs and listened to those rhythms. The reconstruction of the atmosphere of suffering or joy that the ancestors experienced is another way that the ritual can restore the memory of the ancestors and bring forth this component of the self. Growing numbers of African-Americans have made pilgrimages to the slave dungeons in West Africa where the captured Africans were retained while waiting to be shipped to America. The most famous of these sites are Goree Island in Senegal and Elmina and Cape Coast in Ghana. The ability to go into these structures, smell the stench, feel the heat and relive the fear and pain that was endured in these places replays the ancestral tragedy of these places. This experience is not unlike the tribal ritual of the Jewish people who have spent billions of dollars constructing Jewish Holocaust museums around the world and sponsoring tours and rituals of remembering at the sites of Concentration Camps in Europe. This re-living of the deadly experiences of the Jewish Holocaust is an example of Jewish people engaging in an educational ritual that makes them aware of a component of their *tribal ancestral self.* In the education of African-Americans there is a need to institutionalize rituals such as the Holocaust Museum and annual cycles of celebration and active reenactment of the suffering of our ancestors who endured these experiences. The kind of transpersonal sharing that activates this collective hurt goes considerably beyond the recitation of information about slavery and the hurt of that experience. Such shared experiences will help each generation to better grasp the significance of this part of their self. They will gain greater appreciation for the significance of their existence and their relationship to their tribe. It will introduce them to ancestors whose experiences they still share but have no way of knowing. It will help to manifest collective potential left unrealized because of miseducation.

The rituals of remembering are not exclusively for the recognition of hurt and suffering. In fact this aspect of memory is only for the purpose of dramatizing the significance of endurance and survival beyond the event of the trauma. The purpose of educational ritual is not to revel in the past, but as a celebration of the power of overcoming hardship and the resilience of the collective tribal spirit. This shows the real contribution of the ancestors and brings out the inherited potential in each of us that is a consequence of their sacrifice and survival in spite of hardship. In addition to rituals that reenact the hurt of the ancestors, we most have rituals that celebrate and reenact accomplishments of the ancestors. The significance of establishing the Martin Luther King, Jr. holiday was one such event. The courage and commitment of those who struggled for the freedom of the unborn is personified in the life and struggles of Dr. King. He is only one of many thousands of ancestors who gave their lives to insure the progress of freedom. In remembering and celebrating him, we are able to ritualistically invoke the recognition of all of those tribal ancestors who would not give up and struggled to advance freedom for those of us who were not even born at the time of their battles.

Each family and all families of the African-American tribe must incorporate rituals that educate us about this crucial part of our self. The ultimate goal of the rituals is to keep alive the memory of those significant ancestors who opened doors for us. The memory may be kept alive through simple rituals such as maintaining an ancestral wall in the house where pictures of personal ancestors are kept. It may be done through occasional evenings or special holidays when we pull out the scrapbooks and encourage the Elders in the family to share their memories of those who struggled for us. More elaborate ceremonies such as skits during family reunions or story telling during "Homecoming" celebrations can serve to ritualize this important component of educating the tribal self. This education about the tribal self is the way that we access the resource of the endurance, the tie and the continuity that connects us with them and with each other. It's interesting to note with these examples that we must work to expand our notion of education as something beyond the classroom and beyond the usual notion that education is centered around the three R's: "reading, 'riting and 'rithmetic."

In order to achieve the authentic education of African people it is important to understand how African people understand their "self." Once this definition is clear then we can begin to talk about what should take place in the learning process and how it should be done. From this perspective, the idea that education should be "functional" takes on an entirely different meaning. Usually, when a "functional education," is discussed from the European-American perspective, it means that one obtains tools that permit them to get a job and make a living. We are suggesting that a functional education should permit people to know their lives, master their lives and insure the perpetuation of those lives. If this is done, then people are insured of jobs because they will create conditions to insure their survival and continued growth. Once people have self-knowledge they have power to obtain from the world what is needed to insure survival. The nature of **Power** as a dimension of education is the topic of the next section.

KNOW THYSELF

CHAPTER 3

EDUCATION AS POWER

Power is the ability to influence the environment consistent with one's self-interests. It is true that power in this respect carries the implication of domination, but definitely not the domination of other people. This definition of power has implications for the domination or mastery of our needs. Power is intended to put people into the unique position that they can obtain and achieve within the context of their environment those things that maximize their survival and the continuation of themselves to the best of their ability. In a world of plentiful resources as this one is, such power does not require arming oneself as a predator of other human beings. In a world of predators, though, such power would perhaps equip people to adequately defend themselves from becoming prey from the greed of others or to at least seek safe asylum from the predator's oppression. Power in this sense does not require the conquest of other people but only the acquisition of those things which have been realistically assigned for the advancement of ones own people as participants in the human community.

We assume that the environment of the outer world and our inner resources together have all that is needed to insure the comfortable and effective advancement of the human family. We must use our inner resources in order to take from the environment those resources that insure our advancement as human beings. Power then has to do with the relative effectiveness that we have in getting from the environment those things that are in our self-interest. At the simplest level, the environment is the source of food, shelter and clothing that are the fundamental necessities for physical survival. Translated to a broader dimension, all

35

of the resources that are needed for advancement of the physical being are located in the physical environment. The farmer, the scientist, the manufacturer, the banker, the realtor and the stock broker are all engaged in the process of extracting from the physical environment those resources that insure survival and expand a people's control over those resources. Those who have maximum influence over those physical resources are considered to be very powerful. Those who have limited influence are considered weak or certainly, lacking in power. The effect of greed and the drive for domination is that it drives certain people to gain more and more influence so that they can limit the access of other people to these resources in the environment, while maximizing their own access. This is an exploitation of power that is the exaggeration of a natural impulse of self-preservation that becomes the drive for domination rather than participation. What is needed by a people to insure that they are able to eat, are protected against the elements and can defend themselves from danger or disease is nothing magical nor does it require anymore than influencing the environment consistent with our own self interest.

Influencing the Physical Environment

Education is the instrument that should equip people to gain control over the physical resources of the environment. The skills that one develops in the educational environment should maximize each person's ability to gain better access to the resources in their environment. In the highly complex and modern societies, the actual labor of growing food, building houses, creating clothing, discovering new medicines does not depend on individual mastery in these areas. Instead, there is the process of exchange or trade where we give someone something that they need in order to provide us with something that we need. This is what money is about and how the economic process operates. Though these things have been made to appear very complex and abstract, even magical, the bottom line is that people establish mechanisms to insure the survival of themselves and their kind. They are naturally motivated to develop power, i.e., the ability to influence the environment consistent with their own self-interest. A criterion of education then is not how much money that you make, but how effective you are in gaining independent mastery of this power to influence. Are you able to develop such attractive skills or resources that you are always able to negotiate a trade and not depend upon the arbitrary choices of being hired or fired based on someone else's ability to exercise maximum control? So, ultimately, one does not pursue education in order to get a job, but to control resources in such a way that you will always be in a position to negotiate a trade. The Honorable Elijah Muhammad said:

> As a people, we must become producers and not remain consumers and
> employees. We must be able to extract raw materials from the earth

36

*and manufacture them into something useful for ourselves. This would
create jobs in production. We must remember that without land there is
no production. The surplus of what we produce we would sell. This
would develop a field of commerce and trade as other free and independent people . . .*[20]

The slave was removed from the effective negotiation of his/her skills
because their skills belonged to someone else. He could eat if he worked, but he
could also work and not eat depending upon the arbitrary decision of a slave master. Because, the slave had been robbed of access to education, s/he could only
develop the skills that gave their owner the privilege of trade. *"Neo-slavery"* has
provided African-Americans the opportunity to spend a decade in training beyond
secondary school and can only develop skills that permit their "masters" to negotiate a trade. African-Americans become brilliant CPA's who cannot conceive
beyond one of the contemporary "master's" firms. There are brilliant surgeons
who cannot negotiate their skills unless an HMO "master" chooses to bring them
to their plantation. Because we believe that power can only be given as a favor
from a powerful *master,* we fail even to seek the kind of education that effectively empowers us. Too many of the most gifted African-American managers, scientists and manufacturers have no aspiration beyond acceptance on one of the
impressive *plantations* (referred to as "major corporations" or "firms" in modern
language.) Everyone who gets an education cannot become an independent entre-
preneur, but everyone should gain the independent ability to negotiate the trade of
their skills for the necessary resources for survival and advancement. An education that doesn't equip you to do this and ultimately to become an instrument for
the collective advancement of your own community is miseducation in that it
doesn't empower you. Again, as the Honorable Elijah Muhammad observes:

*Since our being brought in chains to the shores of America,
our brain power, labor, skills, talent and wealth have been
taken, given and spent toward building and adding to
the civilization of another people. It is time for you
and me . . . to start doing for ourselves. We must not let
our children be as are we, beggars of another man for his home,
facilities, clothing, food and the means of providing a
living.*[21]

In order to select a proper education rather than training, it is important to
appreciate the goal of education as a device to gain this kind of influences over
the environment. If the end result of education is only to compete for a job rather
than to negotiate for influence then that education has been ineffective. We need
to develop the kind of skills that will bring us autonomy in our immediate environments as individuals and eventually to be a part of a community that has auton-

omy in the world environment. America, Israel, France, etc. must cooperate with other nations in the world for maximum survival and effectiveness but they ultimately approach the world markets with autonomy because they have independent resources to negotiate. This is quite unlike most of the so-called "Third World" nations who are dependent on other nations and international money systems in order to engage in any type of trade. They are therefore, completely at the mercy of those who control those independent systems. The educational systems of so-called "developing" countries should have as their objective the same kind of ultimate autonomy that we are describing here as the goal of education for the African-American.

It is important to remember that autonomy and independence are not terms that mean the same thing as separation and isolation. They mean that you must always interact with others from a position of self-reliance. You can never do all that you need by yourself, but you should always be able to offer those who can do what you need something from your arsenal of capability to fulfill some need that they might have. When you understand that we are all people of a similar destiny, fate and identity and see our cooperation as a necessary part of gaining mutual respect in the larger human arena, then you have come to understand autonomy in the sense that we are describing it here. Autonomy also means cooperation, but it means that you control your own chips in the trade. The laws governing effective cooperation require a moral responsibility to consider the needs of those who share your cooperative unit. If your primary moral demand is to insure your personal success then you are morally liable because you are unlikely to consider the needs of others beyond their ability to fulfill your individual needs. The ultimate result of selfish individualism is a disregard for the needs of other human beings to achieve their human share and a failure to help facilitate that process. In more advanced civilizations, such as the Native Americans and Africans (who actually gave refuge to their conquerors,) there is almost always a strong consideration that each human being will at least have equal access to opportunity. This was the defined agenda of America's *Declaration of Independence* though slavery and the genocide of the Native Americans were blatant contradictions to this claimed agenda.

The Environment of Ideas

We must understand that this "power to influence the environment" is not limited to the physical environment. For the human family, the environment of ideas is even more important than the physical environment. Ideas represent images, concepts, values and all of those things that influence how people think of themselves and the world around them. Those who influence ideas literally control the minds of the people within the environment of those ideas. Our concepts of what's beautiful, what's important, what's news, what's good, what's desirable, etc., are all determined by the environment of ideas. Where people put their energy, their resources, literally, what they do with their lives is determined by the ideas that they internalize. In that we are living in the information age, where our daily experiences are so thoroughly influenced by the media and the ideas that we absorb from it, we are even more subject to the environment of ideas than previous generations have ever been.

Whoever controls ideas can actually manipulate the physical resources of the entire world. An indication of the value of ideas is the fact that advertisers will pay more than $1 million in order to expose their product for less than sixty seconds during a Superbowl game. No one would expend those kinds of resources if they were not aware that they had the power to influence millions of people to want what they have to sell. These companies actually create "wants" and then offer the product to satisfy the want. They are then able to acquire the physical resources of millions, which gives them even greater influence in the material world. There is a genuine understanding that whoever controls ideas, can control whatever they want from the environment. Advertising, marketing, etc., are devices for controlling ideas and manipulating appetites.

The educated person would aspire to gain access to influencing major ideas in the environment. The educated person in communications would not aspire to just sit in front of the camera, but they would want to be the producer in the newsroom where those items that will be reported as news will be selected. They want to be involved in shaping public opinion and not simply reporting those opinions. An "educated" person would want to maximize their control of ideas that are to be communicated because they understand that a real measure of human power is the ability to influence ideas. The kind of influence that properly educated people seek is not the ability to exploit people by enforcing your agenda on them. Instead, the influence of ideas is the way by which people can advance the environment consistent with their self-interest, survival and advancement as human beings. Dr. Woodson states regarding the influence of ideas:

> When you control a man's thinking you do not have to worry about his actions. You do not have to tell him not to stand here or go yonder. He will find his "proper place" and will stay in it. You do not need to send him to the back door. He will go without being told. In fact, if there is no back door, he will cut one for his special benefit. His education makes it necessary.[22]

To be influential simply means to insure that your children will be able maximally to benefit from opportunities that develop their genius and contribute to humanity out of their unique talents. Influence means that your dignity and resources will be respected and you will be capable of developing yourself and your people consistent with the highest human ideals on the planet. Influence means that your perspective will gain a hearing and will be presented before the human family with the same potential impact as the ideas of any other human group. Developing the ability to influence ideas permits you to tell your story to the world and gain the same respect as any other group. The miseducation of African Americans beginning with our captivity, subsequent enslavement and continued oppression has systematically restricted our power to influence ideas. In fact, we have been particularly controlled by the ideas of others that have systematically limited our human effectiveness. Since we have not had access to real education, we have developed faulty ideas about ourselves and do not fully appreciate our capability and human potential. What's even worse is that we have not developed an aspiration to influence ideas, but have comfortably accepted the role of a participant in other's ideas. Our education encourages us to join other people's schools of thought and not to develop our own even when those other schools of thought may have been developed as a tool to insure our continued oppression. Our miseducation results in our participation in other people's environment of ideas with no sense of responsibility to develop our own.

An example of the irresponsibility that miseducated people show to themselves can be seen in the condemnation that has always come to scholars such as Dr. Carter G. Woodson and other so-called "radical" Black scholars. Those thinkers have frequently met with ridicule who have argued that a real education must expose us to ideas about ourselves which inspire us to develop influence in developing ideas which tell *our* story *our* way. Afrocentric thinkers have received broad condemnation because of their commitment to developing influential independent ideas about African people. Such condemnation frequently comes from other African-Americans and is another example of the acceptance of our powerlessness in the environment of ideas.

A true education encourages and empowers people to become influential in the world of ideas. A miseducated person neither develops independent ideas nor a desire to influence the environment of ideas. If a person has not developed the power to influence ideas then their education has not been effective.

Influencing the Societal Vision

Another important aspect of power that comes from proper education is the ability to influence the vision of the society. The vision represents the goals, the agenda and the collective aspirations of the people. The vision raises ones perception from the level of specific ideas to the higher level of ideals. Whereas ideas create the image of how the world exists, the vision creates the image of how the world should be. Here again, the expectation is that people who are appropriately educated would certainly aspire to create a future environment that insured their presence and contribution. People projecting their continued influence across time create this vision. It grows from a sense of the importance of their uniqueness and the value of their continuity. At the physical level, there are few drives that have the intensity of the reproductive drive—that physical urge to perpetuate oneself. Without being told by anyone, normal human beings are driven to continue their lineage beyond their mortal existence. This same drive has a parallel in the arena of ideas and vision. This is the reason that people exert so much energy in the construction of monuments and edifices that they feel will immortalize their ideas for future generations. Every mighty civilization devotes considerable energy to the process of insuring their continuity. In fact, educational institutions themselves are set up, not only to prepare people to preserve the gains of the past, but to insure the continued influence of the present into the future. People write books, develop art works, create images that they hope will preserve their influence on future time.

The desire for immortality ranks high in the religious beliefs of people because they seek to preserve and extend their influence. Education should not only be a device to sustain a people's special vision about the world, but it should equip them to influence the world's vision in very special ways. This is real power when one has developed the capacity to influence the vision of the world. African people have always maintained a vision of the interconnection of human beings and the spiritual significance of all things. This vision is an important one for all humanity and our education should equip us to influence the world in this way.

The African-American victory over the dehumanization of slavery is a testimony to the resilience of the human spirit and the world's vision should be influenced by this example from our experience. The world's vision should be free of the kind of oppression that has characterized European racism and genocidal attacks on groups of human beings based on claims of racial superiority. This influence on the world's vision will not be possible if we are not educated about our experiences and the special contributions that we have made to humanity.

In order to influence the vision, we must have the power of information as well as inspiration. The active work of philosophers, theologians and thinkers in the western world is one of continuously seeking to affect humanity's vision. African-American philosophers, thinkers and artists should seek to influence the vision of the world as well. Those goals of human excellence and moral integrity to which people aspire are defined by the societal vision. As artist seek to create images of beauty and to influence the world to adapt their creative vision, they are exercising the power of shaping the societal vision. Even the desire to engage in vision building is a product of an effective education. Not only should the education equip people with access to their particular vision, but it should empower them to express that vision so that the world will be positively influenced by their creativity.

The power to influence the environment is the most tangible outcome of education. Such power is the result of knowing who you are and what resources are available to you. The reward is the ability to achieve those very things which survival dictates we must all have. The ultimate determination of our successful education is the degree to which we are able to develop power for independent influence. This power should provide us with mastery of sufficient skills to obtain from the physical environment whatever minimal resources we need to insure our survival. We should possess the ability to present ideas about the functioning of the environment and those ideas should bring a positive evaluation of ourselves and enhance our overall effectiveness in the world. Ideas that tell our story, and generate respect for us as a people is the result of effective education. Ultimately, the power that comes from education should well-equip people to participate in structuring the vision that inspires people to reach for greater heights in the advancement of humanity. People who fail to develop this kind of power or who don't want this kind of effectiveness are people who are quite definitely miseducated.

CHAPTER 4

HOW TO STUDY THE SELF

Any discussion of self-knowledge must contain several elements:
1) *Knowledge of the human nature or make up.* This is the study of what constitutes the self. From the perspective of European-American study this includes psychology and the social sciences that we have described in the earlier section in our definition of the Self.
2) *Knowledge of the origins of oneself.* This is usually thought of as the study of the history of oneself as a human being and the development of civilization.
3) *Knowledge of nature, her patterns and the environment in which we live.* This is the study of science and mathematics;
4) *Knowledge of God.* Since life occurs within the context of creation, and Africans agree with most of the human family that we are in the image of God, then knowledge of our Creator is essential to understanding who we are.

Origins of civilization:
The Honorable Elijah Muhammad (1965) stated:

> *To know oneself is to know all men, as from us came
> all and to us all will return.*[23]

The study of the origins of civilized life must begin in the Nile Valley of Africa.

43

Certainly the oldest continuous record of life and knowledge is from this spot in Northern Africa. The continuity of civilization from this place in Africa throughout the civilized world is an important part of this aspect of education. Certainly the study of history and paleontology is a part of this learning. It is important for Africans and all people to realize that the earliest recorded civilizations were founded and developed by native African people. The color of the skin of the Nubians, the Aztec and other pioneers of civilization is certainly not the most important characteristic of these human beings. The significance of their skin color is important only because of a racist miseducation that implied either that all civilization came from white people, or that people of color made no creative contributions to civilized life. Because of this miseducation, ideas of white supremacy can continue to thrive, convincing each new generation of Caucasians that they have an exclusive monopoly on contributions to the development of the planet. It permits Caucasian people to continue to make the claim of a genetically determined inferiority in the intellectual functioning of Black people and a particular gift of genius given to the white people. Claims of this discrepancy continue to emerge from the "loftiest heights" of European American scholarship. Such confidence in Black inferiority is easily accepted when the education of the entire society fails to make note of the fact that the very origins of science and knowledge in every conceivable arena began with the remarkable and well-documented contributions of Black people.

What's even worse is the considerable self-hatred among peoples of color themselves who have no knowledge of their contributions. Again, the Honorable Elijah Muhammad said:

One of the gravest handicaps among the so-called Negroes is that there is no love for self, nor love for his or her own kind. This not having love for self is the root cause of hate (dislike,) disunity, disagreement, quarrelling, betraying, stool pigeons, and fighting and killing one another. How can you be loved, if you have not love for self?[24]

One of the best ways to gain love for self is to gain good knowledge of the positive contributions by ones kind or ones tribal self. It is important for those of European descent to know that a Caucasian man of Europe named Hippocrites made a significant contribution to the development of medicine and is revered in the medical world of the West as the "Father of Medicine." It is even more important that people of African descent know of the Black man called "Imhotep" from Kemit who formulated principles of medicine and was actually worshipped as a deity by Greeks (they called him Asclepius) and the ancient Egyptians. Imhotep lived many centuries before Hippocrites and the medical ethics and techniques that Imhotep had developed no doubt influenced Hippocrites. It is equally significant that Imhotep was a multi-genius excelling as an architect,

44

poet/philosopher, diplomat and advisor to the king. Such genius present in one Black man so long ago immediately raises suspicion about modern claims that Black people are inherently stupid and less capable than white people.

The value of this information is not just for a "feel good" moment, rather it is an essential challenge to the responsibility of those who are inheritors of this legacy of accomplishment. The person who learns about the origins of mathematics, science, astronomy, religion, philosophy, architecture, medicine, etc., all having their origins in the work of African people demands a new level of responsible excellence on the part of African youth. There is no escape from one's ability to excel in any and all fields of knowledge when the young person is able to identify their origins with such models of excellence. They can appreciate that they have the same right and responsibility to be excellent in physics and calculus as they are in basketball and football. Young African Americans find it difficult to achieve at the high levels of academic excellence when the educational system fails to present them with these kinds of models of African excellence.

The importance of "origins" is not only found in the study of the historical record but also in the study of philosophy, language, literature and other aspects of the so-called "Humanities." If we study the development and evolution of language we find very deep "roots" of human thought, again taking us back to Ancient Africa. We discover that most of the symbols and ideas that are claimed as recent have very early origins and have a thread that runs back to the earliest developments of civilized life. We are made to understand that there are no new things, but expanded variations on the old. As awesome as modern technology might be, all of it has humble origins that all members of the human family have made some contribution to. The same is true for the arts that carry symbolic representations of the understandings and perceptions of a "tribe" of humanity. The glorification of the art of European cultures as classical art and the characterization of African Art as "primitive" is another way of reducing the importance of African contributions. People will gain a new level of appreciation for Africa and her genius if they are able to study the true meaning of African Art and the philosophical conceptions that underlie this Art. Not only will this build respect of Africans for themselves, but other people will gain greater respect for African people as well. This is also true of African dance, music, drama etc. As is the case with European dance and drama, there is much to learn about the sensitivity of a people by appreciating their artistic creations and the representation of that Art at the same level of respectability that is attributed by the label of *"Classical"* Art, music, drama, etc.

The growth of civilization is a gradual and cumulative process. Each generation and culture of humanity builds on the discoveries of those who came before them. The truly advanced civilizations of the world have all borrowed from other civilizations and have similarly contributed to subsequent civilizations as a result of their accomplishments. The Nile Valley civilization brought together many of the dispersed accomplishments of a variety of African nations and passed along its achievements to the neighboring Asians and to the Greeks. The Greeks expanded what they learned from the Africans and passed their advances to the Romans who further improved and spread their accomplishments throughout much of the world that we now know as Europe. The process continues and modern European-American civilization represents the result of this evolution. Africa cannot claim the completed form of modern civilization as exclusively her gift, because other cultures have definitely enhanced their contribution. On the other hand, Europe cannot claim an exclusive role as the builders of modern civilization because of their extensive borrowing from other cultures. The reason that the *Study of Origins* is so important is because it shows the continuity of the development of knowledge and how every people have given an invaluable piece to the complex puzzle that is modern life. This study also continues to inspire each new generation to carry-on the tradition that their "tribes" have begun. No one can effectively exclude anyone else from this building process. African young people just like their European counterparts must fully understand the significant role that their people have played in the evolution of civilization. They must then claim their responsibility to continue the process. The cruel injustice of "miseducating" African-Americans has been the deliberate exclusion of their people from the story of the Origins of Civilization. In leaving out the African contribution, recent generations of African people have not been able to assume their responsibility to continue the advancement of the civilization that they started and had made outstanding contributions to, prior to their miseducation.

The Study of Nature

The code and pattern of the Creator's design is found in nature. The best key to understanding our nature is to try to understand the patterns of nature. The various studies of science are the tools for trying to understand the patterns and the workings of nature. The Ancient Africans pioneered the study of the skies in their early work in the study of Astrology. They carefully studied the patterns and the movement of the stars and the heavenly bodies as clues to understanding the changes of the earth. They learned to determine and predict seasons and established calendars based on achieving an understanding of the patterns and cycles of nature. In fact, the understanding that the cosmos operates in a circle (cycle) was one of the essential discoveries about the patterns of life. They began to identify relationships between the patterns of nature and certain characteristics in human beings. It is for this reason that the earliest studies of the heavenly bodies were called *Astrology* rather than Astronomy since the Ancients fully appreciated the relationship between the patterns of nature and certain patterns in human behavior. The same patterns were reflected in their studies of numbers *(Numerology)* and their studies of the principles and processes of transformation that they called *Alchemy*. They understood the principle of transformation to be such a fundamental idea in nature that they devoted considerable study to this principle, again with the objective of better understanding the transformation of the human being. Alchemy as the parent science of Chemistry and Astrology as the parent of Astronomy contained fundamental ideas that reflected the intricate relationship between the patterns of the Earth (nature) and the patterns of the human *Sakhu*[iii] or soul. Education as a method for obtaining knowledge of self must restore its appreciation for the relationship between knowledge of nature and knowledge of self.

The Ancients of the Nile Valley studied the beasts as a means of understanding qualities of excellence that these animals portrayed in their character as symbolic of virtues that humans should strive to develop in their character. Again, the purpose of these studies was to show the relationship between nature and the human self. From the study of the vulture to the study of the beetle, zoology and psychology were intimately connected. The famous representation of the so-called "Sphinx" reflects the intimate relationship between the study of nature and the study of the self. The colossal statue of the Sphinx shows the head of a man affixed to the body of a lion. The lion's nature frequently symbolizes the "King of the Jungle" or a representation of the strength and ferocity of the animal nature. This animal nature was recognized as being a part of the human make-up in our proneness towards impulsiveness, territoriality and even violence. The ancients understood that the reason reflected in the head and face of the human being was the source of mastery over the animal nature. The ferocious nature of the beast is tamed and brought into submission by the power of the human being. This ancient symbol which sits watching the horizon for the daily return of *"Ra"* or the morning sun rising from the East in the Giza desert is a powerful monument to the Ancient understanding of biology, psychology and spirituality as all the same study. The Ancient Africans did not seem oriented towards understanding nature for the purpose of classification and domination, but instead as a means of gaining insight into the human self. Understanding the essential nature of the human being and our relationship to the rest of the cosmos was the major objective of this premiere educational system in the Nile Valley.

The suggestion that is being proposed in this book is that true education must be reconnected with nature as it was done in the ancient Nile Valley. Not only should the study of nature be done as a means of fostering knowledge of self, but also it must be done to teach a respect for nature and the intimate relationship between nature and the human life process. Much of the abuse driven by greed, possessiveness and a fundamental disrespect for nature as literally our "mother," can be attributed to the failure to teach people the relationship between nature and ourselves. We have certainly learned much about how nature works over the last few hundred years of European domination. By learning these things as separate from self-knowledge, we have unleashed more destructive forces than we have

---

[iii] The ancient people of Kemit identified the essence of the human make up as being the soul which they called the Sakhu, This concept is discussed in greater detail in: Akbar, N. (1994) **Light From Ancient Africa**. Tallahassee: Mind Productions & Associates.

discovered humanly constructive forces. The last few generations of human beings led by the scientific revolutions of European knowledge have created more destruction for the earth than all previous generations combined.

Certainly, I do not condemn the contributions that have been made by the development of technology. In fact, we have noted in this discussion that the people of Africa pioneered the earliest forms of technology that went into the construction of the great pyramids and temples of the Nile Valley. The recognition that technology must follow certain patterns of nature and should always be respectful of the intimate relationship between nature and the human self prevented the abuse of nature in the way that it has been systematically assaulted over the last few generations of human life. The African person who learns about nature is constantly reminded that they are learning about themselves. Whether they are studying the laws of physics, the patterns of the plant kingdom, or the movement of the planets, they must maintain a respect that these things are a part of the human self and must be interacted with appropriately. This must be the approach for developing a genuine African-centered education. The study of the earth is approached as a component of the self and with the same values of self-respect and self-direction that guide the study of other components of the self. This does not suggest a sentimental approach to the study of nature that fails to utilize the resources that are useful for our survival, but it does approach the use of nature's resources in a more deliberate and respectful way. For example, we would not leave forests untouched if the lumber is useful for human use, but each generation must seek to replace what they consume for generations yet unborn. This point of view would define the forest as belonging to the "tribe" and not the property of any individual who has the right to exploit its resources. In the tradition of the Native American people and the African people, the land belongs to the community and cannot be bought, sold or owned by any individual.

The other component of nature that is important in understanding the functioning of the self is the study of our physical make-up. We are material creatures as well as spiritual creatures and our physical bodies represent the aspect of nature that is closest to us. So the study of biology, anatomy and physiology is another way that we understand the patterns of nature. The growth, maturation and transformation of our bodies is an important teacher about the processes of spiritual transformation that we cannot see but guide our spiritual progress in a similar fashion. In another of my books entitled **Natural Psychology and Human Transformation,**[25] I offer a lesson on how biology and the study of nature teaches us about our development as spiritual creatures by understanding the patterns that are revealed in the study of the metamorphosis of the butterfly. We use the butterfly as a metaphor to understand the invisible development that takes place in our spiritual evolution.

Our bodies follow certain laws of nature. The way that we eat has a great deal to do with what happens to our bodies. In much the same way, the ideas that we take in have a lot to do with the kind of minds that we develop. Nutrition, exercise and rest are principles necessary for the proper development of the body, but they are also lessons for how we must develop our minds and our spirits. The visible form of the body becomes a way that we can understand the invisible processes of our being. However, the approach to learning about our physical being must keep this relationship in mind. Our bodies, like all other components of our nature, constitute an aspect of who we are and we must see its processes as a means of understanding higher and less visible parts of ourselves.

Another important principle about "correct" education is the idea of "holism." "Holistic education" assumes the interrelationship between all components of nature and not the fragmented and individualized concept that we have learned in the Euro-American approach to education. For example, we know from the study of biology that the body is very much affected by our emotions, and events in our bodies similarly affect our emotions. Our "spirit" of hope and faith also affects what happens to us mentally as well as what happens to us physically. As Western students of healing are just beginning to learn, the state of our minds and spirits have a very direct impact on the state of our health. We cannot separate treatment of the body from treatment of the mind and of the spirit. There is an intimate and inescapable relationship between our mind, body and spirit. As we approach this real education that shields us from "miseducation" we must learn of this relationship and always respect it. The principles that we learn are very valuable in our effort to know ourselves and master ourselves better. We discover, for an example, that our spirit is the most powerful force in our make up. Even though the body follows certain laws of nature, as we described with our discussion of the Sphinx above, the human being is ultimately the master over the flesh. Human reasoning or the mental capacity can stand above the body as the spirit or the soul stands above the mind. The importance of this kind of education is that it helps people to identify where their real power is. When we study our brains and our bodies, we often find ourselves humbled by their impressive capability and will show a tendency to attribute to these marvelous creations greater power to determine our conduct than they deserve. People give greater autonomous power to their bodies than they attribute to the spirits or lives that inhabit those bodies. They are victims of miseducation and are prone to abuse their bodies, ignore their minds and rob themselves of the power that they have over themselves. This is one of the reasons that African-Americans are so often the victims of preventable diseases such as drug abuse, obesity, smoking, lack of exercise. The fact that our miseducation has not informed us of our inner powers, nor respect for those powers or ourselves, leaves us vulnerable to the demands of our lower appetites. Unrestrained appetites for too much of the wrong kinds of foods as well as acquired lusts for chemically created appetites such as drugs, tobacco and alcohol frequently make us victims of our own ignorance of our make-up. This knowledge of who we are and our relationship to nature is one of the ways that we learn to exercise proper authority over our lives and become like the Sphinx, with the human head sitting in control of the ferocious demands of a body like a lion. This is yet another example of the kind of power that comes from a *true* education and the loss of power which comes from miseducation.

The Study of God

This aspect of the education in self-knowledge creates a serious conflict for the European-American educational process. The conflict is a consequence of the rigid separation between "church and state" which has been established in their concept of education. They also maintain a strong separation between the rational and the spiritual that actually fuels a continuing conflict between spiritual and scientific knowledge. As we noted in our discussion above regarding the "study of nature" as an aspect of self-knowledge, such a conflict does not exist in our model of education. The model that we are presenting already assumes a spiritual or divine core in the make up of the human being. In fact, as we have noted above, you cannot study the nature of the human being without studying the spiritual nature. So this model of education that is holistic must respect the soul as being as much a part of our nature as is the body. When we identify the soul, we are automatically in a discussion about a reality that transcends matter and time and places us in a spiritual domain. We have in this acknowledgement invited God into our studies.

This African concept of God's presence is different from the European-American concept of "Theology" or the study of religion. The European-American culture considers the study of God as a separate discipline and a force separate from and independent of the physical and rational life of the human being which one may choose to believe or not. There are certainly many European-American Theologians and Believers in religion who do not make this kind of separation, but the collective worldview of the culture maintains a separation between the "secular" and the "sacred." The African concept of life and its concept of education require that the sacred and the secular should be seen as one. The African worldview does not approach the study of God as some kind of force independent of the human reason and physical reality. Instead it sees God as an inescapable component of the human life. As we noted above, this approach to education studies nature or science as the language of the Creator and therefore there is no argument about creation as taught in religious dogma versus theories of science. The African accepts that God did the creation and there is respect for science's efforts to understand how God did it. There is no attempt to find in history a preserved footprint of God's presence, but there is an assumption that wherever there is life, there is God. This means that science is the study of God and history is the study of God, because each of these aspects of the self represents dimensions of God's expression in the human make-up. One need not have a war of religious dogma in order to discuss the ontological inescapability (definite and unquestioned being) of God in the African conception of life. Creation is proof of the existence of the Creator. The maintenance of life is verification of the continued influence of that Creator. Ultimately, the human being's discovery of him/herself is the most certain proof of the reality of God.

Because of the Euro-American separation of the material and the spiritual and the willingness to discuss God only in relation to religion, this aspect of education becomes rather difficult within the confines of their current worldview. As one develops a curriculum in the study of the African self, there is a natural requirement to study God. We have discussed already issues such as components of the self (which begins with the Soul, the Divine presence in the human makeup) and the importance of moral instruction as an essential part of this African educational system. We find instruction about God in every aspect of the *true* education that we are describing in this discussion. Even our discussion of science requires us to study nature as an expression of the Creator and therefore, to learn science is to learn the way that God expresses Itself. From this point of view, the study of physics, biology, chemistry or mathematics is actually the study of God within an integrated approach. Such an approach minimizes the dogma that is attached to religion and the various religious descriptions of the nature of God. Instead, one is invited to discover the nature of God through God's own creation and through self-knowledge one becomes acquainted with God from the vantage point of God's highest creature—the human being.

Again this is consistent with the way of the Ancient African people who studied and expressed God in all that they did from their language, to their art, to their monuments and buildings. All of traditional African culture maintains this implicit presence of God that does not require an independent religious expression to affirm and know God. Instead, all of the life of the traditional African is understood as an expression and communication with God. Certainly, most African people in contemporary times also practice one of the world's great religions, whether it's Islam or some form of Christianity. In the traditional cultural life of the African, God is always assumed to be present and worshipped in every aspect of ones life. What appears to be a religious preoccupation or even fanaticism on the parts of so many African people as they practice the Judeo-Christian-Islamic religions is a consequence of a "Tribal" consciousness that already has God in the center. It is almost redundant to say that an African person is "religious" if one means by religion that one is affirming of God, since the African person by virtue of the core of their being (the Soul) is an affirmation of God.

In order to comfortably rethink a proper education that reflects the African person's concept of God requires a thorough rethinking of how the world is seen through the eyes of African people. This is a difficult task for the miseducated African person or certainly for someone who is evaluating this system from the European-American perspective that is by its very nature dualistic. This duality approach suggests that the concept of God is a separate reality overseen by religious systems and ideas and the non-religious world is under the authority of the scientist, politician or academician. The "separation of Church and State" is not just a political value, but is the very essence of a view of the world that sees the spiritual world as a world separate and apart from the material world. Of course, when the two (religious and secular) worlds are fused one discovers real confusion and contradictory postures such as in the case of the "Religious Right" in the U.S.A. that condemns abortion while failing to support projects that prevent the starvation and neglect of poor children who are alive. In the Islamic world, we find zealots who seek to reintegrate politics and religion and end up killing innocent people to demonstrate their demand to create a "moral" religious state rooted in the spiritual ideas of the **Holy Qur'an** which condemns killing the innocent.

The African synthesis of spirituality in the material environment is a lesson that needs to be modeled for the entire world. Africans in the traditional practice of their culture experience no contradiction between their spiritual awareness and their governmental awareness. The two worlds appear to operate quite compatibly so long as the way of approaching the world is one rooted in the African view of reality.

It is critical that one must adopt an African perspective in order to integrate this spiritual component into one's educational system. In a non-African context, the teacher might find him/herself guilty of a criminal offense by violating the separation of church and state. An interesting example of this dilemma is the way that the ban against school prayer has operated for African-Americans. This has been an area of great controversy with law suits and militant reaction to the ban within the European-American community. In environments where African-Americans did not have the interference of European-American people, school prayer has continued uninterrupted. This is true in the classroom, on the football field and at any ceremonial occasion where African-Americans are responsible for the planning of the program. This uncontested religious expression has continued despite considerable religious diversity within the African-American community. The only group without an identifiable representation in the African-American community is the atheist. All kinds of Protestant and Catholic Christians abound within the African-American community as do Muslims, Hebrews, Rastas and a variety of African traditional religions, but there has been no protest of the practice of calling for prayer in nearly any formal gathering of African-Americans.

This phenomenon has been suspiciously undiscussed. One reason that it has not been discussed is that there is a tacit understanding that the African concept and experience of God and religion is quite different from the European one. The centrality of God in the life space of Africans is intense and non-debatable. Africans overwhelmingly accept the reality of God without question. There is no uniformity as to how one should acknowledge, worship or identify that God, but God's reality goes pretty much uncontested throughout the African world. This kind of consensual acceptance of spiritual assumptions in the African worldview is why I am suggesting that in order to effectively synthesize the study of God with the general educational experience it would be necessary to operate in an

African-based environment. Otherwise, we would find this discussion able to occur only in settings that had been legitimized by some particular religious community and perspective. The context for the study of God that is being suggested in this section is not an excuse to proselytize for a particular religious view, but the need to understand the reality of God as a part of the educational process. When we realize that many of the images and concepts in traditional religion have been contrary to the success of people of color, it becomes even more important why the study of God should not be the study of religion. For example, so many of the images associated with Christianity are reflective of European projections of themselves on the leading figures of the religion. It has been rather comical to see some African-American converts to Far Eastern religions attempt to look "appropriate" by trying to grow a single pigtail with hair that such a style would not easily accommodate to. The same is true with the strong confusion of the practice of Islam with the traditional Arab culture and the perception that one must dress in traditional Arab desert dress in order to be authentic in ones practice of the religion. The confusion of an alien culture and races with the concept of the religion will only serve to further miseducate us as we identify with the outer expression rather than with the inner Truths of the religions.

It is important to emphasize that the study of God as a component of the person's self-knowledge is not intended to create or perpetuate religious ideology. It is clear that religious discussion and debate has a place in the educational process, particularly for those who are committed to developing effective rituals and disciplines consistent with the spiritual advancement of people. As we have noted above, such assumptions about the spiritual expression and development of the person are very much consistent with an African-based educational system that assumes the spiritual nature of people. However, even in traditional African practices there is considerable variation in how the process of spiritual development should be approached, and how people should reconcile themselves with the spiritual world and with the Transcendental Being. The study of God should provide people with evidence of the reality of God and the relevance of Higher Spiritual forces in their lives. The student should emerge from this aspect of their learning with an appreciation for the kind of order, precision and certainty that exists in the creation. With respect for such order, there is the appreciation for an "Ordering Force," which is usually acknowledged as God. How one chooses to identify, reverence or even develop a relationship with this Being should remain a part of the very personal religious choices that people make. "There should be no compulsion in religion," declares the **Holy Qur'an.**[26] There should be, however, an acknowledgement and respect for the religious life of people. Perhaps, the study of various ways that people identify and reverence God would be an appropriate component of this study of God. The study should avoid the constraint that comes when you seek to recruit people into a particular religious method while respecting all ways that people acknowledge the reality of a Higher Being. Such acknowledgement is a critical part of the self-knowledge of the human being educated in an African system of learning. The study of these areas of knowledge should serve as the foundation for studying the self. It's important to recognize that we do not discard any knowledge. In the use of the Western language, we have included the physical and social sciences, mathematics, literature, religion, etc. Any knowledge that is of Truth has relevance in the education of the African person. How these areas are studied and their relationship to each other is dictated by the African worldview. This is the point of difference when we begin to discuss educating African people about themselves. Certainly, there are many aspects of this study that would be relevant to all human beings, but our objective is neither to proselytize nor to impose our worldview or culture on others. The intention is simply one of identifying our approach and suggesting that the only proper education for us is one that is based on our worldview. So the nature of the self, the origins of life, the study of the processes of life and the study of the Creator of life are the essential content for our education. Implicit in this model is a correction for the processes that perpetuate miseducation and make us enemies of ourselves.

CHAPTER 5

LEARNING TO EDUCATE OURSELVES

Once we know what a real education is and understand what it is supposed to do, then an important question is, "How do we learn to educate ourselves?" One of the real problems that results from "miseducation" is not only the absence of effective information to empower ourselves, but not even knowing how to go about the process of educating ourselves. As I have discussed above, the educational process that was designed for African-Americans was never intended to prepare us for independence and self-determination, but to perpetuate our servitude to people who already have power. In the previous sections I have described what should be the content of an effective education for self-knowledge. In this final section, I want to identify the methodology that should be used for the process of educating ourselves.

W. Curtis Banks[27], in an important discussion describing the development of Black Psychology identified a very similar problem to the one that we have identified as existing in the education of African-Americans. This problem was the failure of European-American psychology to offer the kind of understanding and approach that would permit it to effectively improve the lives of Black people. Dr. Banks identified three critical methods in this development of Black Psychology. These methods were: *deconstructionist, reconstructionist* and *constructionist*. These rather big terms have simple meanings and a great importance to our learning of how to educate ourselves.

55

Deconstruction

The *deconstructionist* approach is intended to critique or identify the error and weaknesses found in the typical approaches to education for African-Americans. Much of the preceding discussion in this book has utilized the deconstructionist approach in its description of the limitations of the Euro-American approach to teaching non-European people. Even the concept of "miseducation" by Dr. Woodson, which has served as the foundation of much of our discussion, is based on this approach which identified what is wrong with the educational experience of African-American people. Even though the majority of our discussion has emphasized the flaws in this system, as it impacts on African-Americans, we have been careful to indicate that many of those flaws become assets in the process of bringing European-American people into knowledge of themselves.

Deconstruction is the necessary first step in the re-educational process of African-Americans because of the extensive influence of the European-American methods and ideas of education. Those methods and ideas, as we have noted, were intended to advance the self-knowledge and power of people of European ancestry. The intention was never to educate people of non-European ancestry about themselves. It was stated in the legal documents that established segregation in the educational system that this system was not set up for non-white people in America. Not only was the system set up for "White Only," non-white presence was not even welcomed in the same building where education was going on. Though such formal and legal segregation was not always enforced in the Northern part of the United States, *de facto* segregation achieved the same exclusionary objective. This "White only" educational system was never altered even when African-Americans were admitted into the European-American system. As a result, much of what we have learned educationally, is based on methods and ideas intended to advance the self-knowledge of European-descended people. Most of these ideas must be "deconstructed." (We prefer this term from Dr. Banks rather than "destroyed" because it permits us to make a systematic analysis of what is usable and what is not; what is included for the educational advancement of European people and what is "actual fact.") The deconstruction process permits us to pick-and-choose based on our redefinition of education in order that we may understand the educational process that European people have used for themselves and at the same time identify those things that have inhibited our educational development.

Most of the discussions by African-American scholars intent upon improving the education of their people in the last quarter of the twentieth century have been primarily of a deconstructionist nature. African-American and other ethnically (and gender) distinct scholars who have taken up this challenge have basically contended that the educational ideas in the American educational system have excluded the non-European contributions and approaches to understanding the world. These numerous scholars have argued for Black Studies, Native American Studies, Latino Studies, Asian Studies, and Women's studies as an effort to address these distortions in a Eurocentric, male-centered approach found in most educational settings. They have argued (as has been repeatedly suggested in this volume) that education in America has been built around a set of goals which advanced white and male supremacy. The deconstructionist must address these limitations in traditional European-American education. Many African and African-American thinkers (such as Molefi Asante, Yosef ben-Jochannan, John Henrik Clarke, Cheikh Anta Diop, Asa Hilliard, John G. Jackson, Maulana Karenga, Wade Nobles, Ivan Van Sertima, Chancellor Williams and many others) have consistently addressed the historical omissions that have excluded us from the world's stage. The Europeanizing and whitening of Africa (particularly Nile Valley Civilization) has been a major point of interest in their discussions. The deconstructionists have attempted to discard those distortions of history, which have failed to address the contributions of African people. Similarly, the early deconstructionists from the first half of this century such as Carter G. Woodson, J.A. Rogers, George G.M. James and others sought to point out how African people had been omitted as contributors to human progress.

Deconstruction is the necessary first step towards the education of African people who have already been miseducated by a European-American educational system. Since so much of our information (even the language that we use) has come to us through European systems, we must carefully scrutinize the information that we are using. It is critically necessary to realize that something is wrong with our training before we can even begin to address what is needed for our re-education. When we have been miseducated, we have been implanted with a defense of what has been learned. It may be possible to raise some occasional questions about the information that we have obtained, but it is extremely difficult for a person to acknowledge a rather comprehensive flaw in their learning experiences. It is like trying to appreciate the concept of color when one is genetically color-blind. The Euro-centric educational system has so thoroughly excluded realities about people of color that we are often handicapped in our ability to see non-white accomplishment. This has infected us with a kind of academic colorblindness and we don't even know that we are. From this point of view, many of the uneducated or poorly educated offer the least resistance to the need for deconstruction. Perhaps, this is why the radical reform advocated by important African-American Community leaders such as Marcus Garvey and Elijah Muhammad appealed to this group of the minimally miseducated. The so-called "marginal" members of the African-American overwhelmingly populated Marcus Garvey and Elijah Muhammad's self-help movements. It is equally interesting to note that the strongest resistance to the call for independent thought, self determination and independent education came from those who were "trained the most." Elijah Muhammad proclaimed:

My people should get an education which will benefit their own people and not an education adding to the "storehouse" of their teacher.

57

*We need education, but an education which removes us from the shack-
les of slavery and servitude. Get an education, but not an education
which leaves us in an inferior position and without a future. Get an
education, but not an education that leaves us looking to the slave-
master for a job.*[28]

Of course, Elijah Muhammad received the same kind of opposition from
the highly miseducated that Marcus Garvey received from representatives of the
educational establishment, such as Dr. W.E.B. DuBois. Dr. DuBois eventually
adopted many of the perspectives of Garvey after going through the "deconstruction" process himself. This kind of opposition is certainly expected from people
who have not undergone the deconstruction process. This is why the first step in
learning to educate ourselves requires us to go through this process of looking at
what we have learned, identifying its flaws and eliminating those parts which perpetuate our miseducation. Once we have become miseducated, we believe what
we have learned and become proud defenders of its "truth" even if it requires us
to argue for our own inferiority as many of our African-American scholars have
done. Of course, they do not claim that they are inferior, but suggest their superiority to be directly proportional to the degree to which they have internalized and
acted upon European American standards of excellence and competence. Once
they have gone through the process of deconstruction, they are better equipped to
purge themselves of the self-destructive ideas that fail to empower them and com-
pel them instead to maintain white empowerment.

Reconstruction

The *reconstructionist* approach is the next stage in this process of learning to educate ourselves. The reconstructionist is devoted to correcting the errors
in Euro-American education and re-building it into a model more sensitive and
relevant to the previously excluded group. The approach of this methodology
goes one step beyond the criticism and description of the problems found in the
deconstructionist approach, and begins the process of trying to build a corrected
educational system. Though it is still building from the context of what is wrong,
the emphasis is shifted to how to make things right. The two methods are not
mutually exclusive, and certainly reconstuctionism grows out of the critique of
the deconstructionist's approach. Reconstructionism is primarily a corrective
approach that is very sensitive to the inaccurate information and approaches that
have been discovered through the deconstructionist phase.

An excellent example of the reconstuctionist's approach is the work of
Dr. Ivan Van Sertima, particularly in his important work entitled **They Came
Before Columbus.**[29] Dr. Van Sertima joins with the deconstructionists in chal-
lenging the mythology of a European "discovery" of America in 1492. The deconstructionists argue that the account of this story fails to take account of the inhabitants who occupied this land at the appearance of the Europeans. It also com-

pletely omits the idea that people from Africa had come to this part of the world as early as 700 B.C.E.[iv] and afterwards around 1300. Van Sertima brings forth considerable evidence to substantiate this claim that is so blatantly absent in the Eurocentric description of the founding of America. His approach is reconstructionist because it begins to introduce new data that is sensitive to the omissions that have distorted history and feed the process of miseducation.

Another example of the reconstructionist's approach is the outstanding work of the Senegalese multi-scholar, Dr. Cheikh Anta Diop. Dr. Diop's important work, **The African Origin of Civilization: Myth or Reality**[30] challenges the claim that Nile Valley civilization was built by people other than native inhabitants of Africa (i.e., Black people.) In his re-building of the story of history, he presents compelling evidence that has been ignored in the European-American version of the development of world civilization. Using evidence of paleontologists, linguists, microbiologists and a variety of other fields of study, he makes a compelling argument for human civilization having its origin in Africa and being transported across the Mediterranean into Greece and other parts of the world. Again, this kind of research and scholarship is typical of the work of the reconstructionist who is trying to develop an educational system that addresses those facts that include African people in the development of civilized life. His work is also typical of the reconstructionist in that he utilizes a lot of the data that would be compelling to a skeptical European audience. He has to utilize many of the references and the type of concrete empirical data that is likely to be convincing to Europeans looking at the world from their point of view. This is another of those instances where the "miseducational" process, though limited in its contribution to independent African development, it is valuable by informing the African scholar how the Europeans are likely to interpret information and what kind of information would be most effective in navigating through barriers that their education has constructed

Basically, reconstruction is the next necessary phase in this process of learning how to educate ourselves. It is not sufficient to just point out what's wrong in the miseducational system—it is necessary to do the research that begins to set the record straight. As I have noted throughout this discussion, it is not possible to have functional self-knowledge unless we begin to know facts about ourselves. The reconstructionist scholar and educator makes a conscious and deliberate effort to dig up the hidden facts and develop a compelling argument that begins to include those crucial pieces, which have been excluded from the miseducational system. This second phase is also the student's next step in correcting their miseducation. Once the student has been made aware of the flaws and fallacies in the miseducational system by exposure to the ideas of deconstructionists, they must begin to reconstruct and fortify their education by studying the work of the reconstructionists. In other words, once we know that our history and

---

[iv] Before the Christian Era.

experiences have been excluded from the learning environment, we must begin to supplement our learning in order to locate the pertinent information about ourselves.

Another important component of the reconstructionist's approach is to operate with the express objective of providing information that will liberate the African-American mind. This means that the educational information is intended to provide the learner with an aspiration and understanding of what it means to be a free people. Whereas miseducation fosters a dependency on others and disrespect for the autonomy of the oppressed group, the reconstructionist is committed to developing ideas that demonstrate the ability of the group to conduct themselves as an independent group among other independent groups of human beings. They must help the learner to understand that they historically have been capable of doing those things for themselves that insure survival. Despite their long-term oppression, they are still capable of engaging in independent self-determined activity. The ability to develop resources, define reality, defend ones community, etc., are some of the rights that all humans possess but cannot execute unless they have been educated into self-knowledge. The ability to break away from many of the practices that were developed under the conditions of slavery can only occur when one has been mentally liberated which is a part of what must come from the information and the techniques identified by the reconstructionists.

Prior to the latter half of the 20th century there was not a lot of information in this regard because despite the protests of a few scholars such as Dr. Carter G. Woodson in the early part of this century, the concept of miseducation was not widely accepted. As a result of the Civil Rights era of the mid 20th century, an increasing number of African-American scholars became a part of the ranks of the deconstructionists. Over the last quarter of the 20th century, the work of the deconstructionists has both grown and given birth to a large number of reconstructionists. The combined contribution of the work from these two approaches has greatly expanded the consciousness of the existence of "miseducation " and the data for the process of re-education. At the end of the 20th century, fewer people will challenge the fact that the European-American system miseducates non-European (non-white) descended people. There are a growing number of people who have been exposed to the kind of information that is leading them towards a functional and correct education. There are not yet enough reconstructionists and even fewer reconstructionist institutions that can effectively offer an alternative education for the real empowering self-knowledge of African-American people. Schools such as the independent African-American schools found in Washington, DC, Detroit, Chicago and other major cities are still too small and too rare. The African-American Male Academies founded in the late 1980's in Detroit and Milwaukee have had astounding success in offering a positive education in self-knowledge, but it's almost too little too late for the thousands of African-American young people that we are continuing to lose as we enter the New Millenium.

Though many of the sources and the scholars who are reconstructionists are under attack with the growing swing to Right Wing conservatism in the U.S.A., these scholars have been very successful in ushering in a new reconstructionists era. Organizations such as the *"Association for the Study of Classical African Civilization,"* **The Journal of Black Studies** and **The Journal of Black Psychology** and many other documents have effectively dispersed the message of reconstructionism throughout the world. There is a growing body of information that presents the reconstructionist's data.

Construction

The third methodology described by Dr. Banks in this development of a self-serving approach to knowledge is the *constructionist* approach. Wade Nobles[31] also uses the Banks model in his description of the development of "African Psychology." Nobles suggests that the constructionist approach "reflects the belief that work found in the field (of African Psychology) must result in simultaneously promoting the welfare of Black people and advancing the critical growth of knowledge." This approach maintains the objectives of the preceding approaches of deconstruction and reconstruction because it remains committed to the conscious and deliberate development of knowledge that promotes the welfare of Black people. This is a clear and deliberate condition for the educational process for self-knowledge that we are discussing. As I have established in the preceding chapters, if the education does not enhance the well being of the people involved in the process, then we cannot accurately identify it as education.

The constructionist approach goes a step further than the preceding approaches, in that it seeks to *advance the critical growth of knowledge*. This goal does not preclude the work of the deconstructionist who offers a critique of the exclusions and oversights of the existing knowledge base. This deconstructionist's critique offers insight into the inaccuracies in the existing knowledge and invites continued review and discussion of ideas. From this point of view the deconstructionist approach represents a significant contribution to the growth of knowledge. Knowledge must ultimately expand our grasp of the Truth and the identification of untruths (either by commission or omission) as it assists us in our understanding. Certainly the reconstructionist approach provides a great contribution to the advancement of understanding by offering new information that has been excluded or distorted in the existing educational arena

In addition to continuing down the path of these earlier two approaches, the constructionist assumes a particular responsibility to develop a synergy that tries to counter earlier errors, remain true to the particular interests of a specific group of learners and offer a balanced perspective that permits knowledge to grow. The ideas of Eurocentric education, critiqued through the educational ideas of the deconstructionists, modified by the information offered by the reconstructionists and ultimately brought into balance with a more "universal perspective" offered by the constructionists offers a holistic contribution through these studies.

Cedric Clark (a/k/a/ Syed Khatib)[32] in his classical essay found in the first edition of the Jones volume **Black Psychology,** states: "The tasks for Black Studies as I see it, then, is to describe the nature and limitations of 'classical' social science and, at the same time, develop a framework within which 'modern' social science can develop and hopefully flourish." It seems that the role of the constructionist's educational approach is very much in the orientation described by Clark.

The constructionist comes to the table aware of the problems of provincial or ethnocentric approaches to education since they have had to master this kind of approach that excluded them in the Euro-American educational system. Such educators are, by their own admission, miseducated. The motivation for their work in attempting to develop an appropriate educational system for Black people is their own miseducation. They are, therefore aware of the assets and the liabilities of the existing knowledge. This means that they are in a unique position, not only to critique what already exists but also to build a fair and equitable approach to education that includes them but does not repeat the errors that gave birth to their condition of miseducation. The constructionists are able to bring something to the arena of ideas that the Eurocentric education does not have: a perspective on the limitations of excessive self-knowledge. The educator who remains with the deconstructionist's approach can ultimately only perpetuate the limitations that already exists in the system that they are deconstructing. If the reconstructionists only address their particular presence and role in the world's knowledge, then they will create a mirror image of the Eurocentric system that currently focuses only on the European experience and contributions. The constructionist is able to bring the best from both the Eurocentric and Afrocentric perspectives while at the same time providing a kind of synthesis that ultimately advances knowledge as a more accurate portrayal of what is Truth.

For example, the fallacy of describing the founding and development of America as an exclusive European activity is well critiqued by the deconstructionists. The introduction of information by the reconstructionists that permit us to see the African presence preceding the landing of the Europeans on this continent expands our awareness of what is obviously true. It accounts for the evidence of African presence in Central and South American preceding the coming of Columbus in 1492. The learned vigilance of the constructionist permits them to reflect on the African contribution but to be careful to include the Native American contributions. It is important to respect the Native American cultures as extensions of the great Mayan and Aztec civilizations. What has been dismissed as savagery, primitiveness or other degrading designations emerges as the aboriginal foundation of what is truly American culture. It also brings to the table of ideas an awareness of the genocidal precedents that led to the establishment of modern America. The possibility of cleansing the U.S.A. of this deadly moral flaw in the fiber of its foundation is a critical necessity in order for healing to take place. Despite, these critiques there are no efforts to deny the considerable positive contributions that have come from the European presence in America. This type of analysis can only come from the kind of educational system that is able to see broadly from more than one perspective of self-knowledge. Ironically, only those who have gone through the process and have been effectively deconstructed have this perspective.

Similarly, the constructionist's approach requires a critique of the roots of one's real self. The kind of human miseducation that permitted Africans to participate in the enslavement of their own people and to fall victim to the materialistic offers of the invaders must be critiqued. There is certainly much greatness about Africa that must be told in this reconstructionist's education, but much must be explained about the downfall of Africa. Where was the vulnerability and what role did the limitation of African self-knowledge play in the defeat and victimization of Africa? If European power was great enough to take us without any resistance on our part, then we need to understand and perhaps adopt the European approach to knowledge. But, if there were things in our own human development that were flawed then the constructionist should help us to better understand those limitations and offer us an arena for greater growth. If we can master these limitations in our own development, then we are best equipped to make some very unique contributions to the development of knowledge for all of humanity.

It is through the constructionist that new approaches or paradigms are introduced to the field of knowledge. The new approaches of education that should emerge from the constructionists of Black education should not only enhance the education of African-American people, but it should offer some new and more effective models for the education of people in general. One example of this possible improvement might be in the area of moral development. As I mentioned in Chapter 2, the education of African children has always included moral instruction as a part of the holistic development of people. At a time when there is considerable concern about the moral development of all children in the educational system, there are certainly concepts from the holistic African paradigm that could benefit all students in the U.S.A. This is an example of how a contribution to the overall growth of human knowledge is made from the constructionist's approach.

Another objective for the constructionist is to offer an orientation and encourage the development of institutions that perpetuate the developing ideas that have come from the reconstructionists and from their work. The constructionists must be institution-builders because they must maintain the independent knowledge base that has emerged from the evolution of their approach. They must have independent institutions that generate ideas, distribute them and maintain them. The constructionists then must advocate and work towards developing "Think Tanks" for the development of new ideas, laboratories for the exploration of these ideas and publications for the dissemination of these ideas. There must be schools and settings where these ideas can be effectively communicated without the interference of alien funding and controlling forces. So, an important part of what the constructionists must do is to create methods for generating wealth that will provide the kind of independent funding that will let such institutions exist and thrive. The constructionists must address whatever political and economical tools might be necessary to maintain the self-sufficiency of such independent institutions. Without such institutions, the work of the constructionist is of no significance. It is the constructionist who ultimately must pioneer the new institutions that provide the shelter for the deconstructionist and the reconstructionist who will ultimately be unable to survive in the old institutions, that their work requires them to condemn. Many great philanthropists have supported institutions of learning such as Universities and settings such as libraries and great museums. These great men and women of wealth understood that their alliance with the constructionists preserved their wealth and power for even unborn generations, because by preserving ideas and education, one is able to maintain power in perpetuity for one's kind. The constructionist must identify ways so that holders of wealth within their own communities will obtain the kind of education into self-knowledge that will make them supporters of such innovative institutions. Unfortunately, most of the non-white holders of such great wealth in the contemporary society have been able to secure their wealth and influence by successfully applying their miseducation. In doing so, they have achieved great influence but they only perpetuate the power and influence of those people who are responsible for their miseducation.

These techniques for learning to educate ourselves that we have discussed in this chapter are important criteria for setting up our educational system. Such a system must contain elements that address each aspect of these techniques. Miseducated African-Americans (and other historically oppressed groups as well) must be systematically introduced to ideas that deconstruct their miseducation. The curriculum must have components that deconstruct those concepts that are destructive to ones effective development and empowerment. A part of this technique is to offer an honest appraisal of what is ones self interest. For African-Americans this means that students must know the painful and unpleasant facts of how we came to be Americans and how the majority of our time has been spent in America. This is a violent and barbaric story that probably offends the sensitivities of some who feel that such a story of murder, plunder, rape and exploitation is not appropriate for the young and even some of the old. To understand this story of America's historical relationship to people of African descent is necessary to create a context for what constitutes our unique educational needs. Of course, such horror stories are not unique to the African-American experience and this deconstructionist's technique is an important part of Jewish education as they learn about their holocaust experience in Europe that sets a context for appropriate Jewish education. Horrible though it may be, there is no hesitation in describing early and thoroughly what the outcome of Jewish persecution has been. Certainly, there is no reason why people of African descent should not know about the atrocities of their experiences in order to understand the importance of a special education for themselves.

Certainly for all of the reasons that we have discussed in the preceding chapters, the reconstructionist's approach must bring to bear that special and unique knowledge that leads to self-knowledge. We must know our unique and special story in order to be effectively educated and this is the major focus of the reconstructionist's approach. Certainly the expansion from our particular story to the universal story of all humanity is the ultimate responsibility that our education must afford, and this becomes the role of the constructionist who begins to integrate our unique experiences into the universal human experience. With our understanding of the universal human experience there must be a universal standard of what is in fact civilized and morally correct human conduct that goes beyond the standards of any particular cultural context. This is a part of the search for Universal Truth, that is a part of the task for the constructionist. The application of these three techniques opens the door to learning how to educate ourselves.

CONCLUSION

The way that a people think and consequently how they act is a product of what they "know." The knowledge that a people receive is a consequence of their education. This discussion has joined the chorus of distinguished Thinkers and Activists who have argued for nearly a hundred years that the persistence of many self-destructive and non constructive behaviors within the African American community is a result of the kind of thinking that has not been inspired by our self-interest. Dr. Carter G. Woodson's simple little masterpiece entitled, **The Miseducation of the Negro,** has become the classic document that describes the origin of this thinking. Dr. Woodson's claim that African Americans have been "educated" out of their own self interest is a position that has grown in acceptance despite its early rejection by many African-American and certainly most, European-American scholars. Dr. Woodson recognized that the thinking that kept most African Americans working to advance the cause of non-African people and systematically sabotaging their own success, was a consequence of the kind of knowledge that we had. Perhaps, if his call had been heeded in the 1930's when it went out, we would not have spent most of this century "chasing ideas that were not our own."

The under-appreciated, but highly successful social and religious movement directed by the Honorable Elijah Muhammad was another powerful example of the call for African Americans to develop "self-knowledge," as the necessary prerequisite for changing our lives and changing our communities. Though this call and analysis did not come from the academy as did Dr. Woodson's, it too fell on deaf ears among the majority of the African-American community and was summarily condemned by almost all of the non-African world. The unprecedented reformations, transformations and developments that Elijah Muhammad achieved with his work in the Nation of Islam well demonstrated the highly successful consequence of applied "knowledge of self." Certainly, his approach and his metaphors were highly unusual, but the foundation of his approach was a defiant conviction to be self-determining and committed to the re-education of the African-American person. Though he achieved considerable economic success and institution building, the most impressive outcome was the solid and meaningful personal reform that was brought about in the lives of the adherents to Mr. Muhammad's movement. The fact that his movement was able to take destroyed and misdirected lives that had been thrown away to vice, criminality and personal self-destruction and to convert those lives to responsible and constructive social contributors was nothing short of miraculous. Though the movement was ideologically and structurally very complex, the fundamental concept that guided everything else in the philosophy was the importance of "self-knowledge" as the key to transforming human life.

This discussion has identified some of the critical elements involved in "self-knowledge." I have looked at the ancient directive from the Nile Valley Civilization: "Man, know thyself!" and pointed out the significance of this simple but profound dictum. Education is identified as the vehicle by which consciousness or knowledge is transmitted. The distinction between training and education being that the latter is successful in formulating a meaningful identity, initiating the learner into their unique human legacy, and involving them in the formulation of a shared vision. Self-knowledge is not possible until we are clear as to what the "self " is. The particular understanding of the self from the vantagepoint of traditional African thought was a key component to our formulation of how to develop this effective and relevant knowledge of self.

Anyone committed to the effective improvement of the lives of human beings in general and of African-American lives in particular must always deal with the vexing question of "so what?" Is the discussion just one that is supposed to be philosophical, entertaining or provocative or is it supposed to make a real difference in the social and personal lives of people. The "so what?" question for this definition of education is answered in the description of education as power. It is precisely this education that is described as "self-knowledge," that empowers people to influence the environment to produce those necessities that insure their advancement as a people and heals those disabilities that interfere with this advancement. "So what?" With a proper understanding of what education is and then the acquisition of that education, we become more than acceptable vehicles for the advancement of other people's objectives, but we cast ourselves in starring roles on the stage of human progress.

In the description of the content and process for self-education, I provide specific guidelines for the development of an authentic education system that achieves for disempowered people the same ends that education achieves for people with power. This is not intended to be a document to advocate for the establishment of an "Afrocentric" or separatist educational system. It is intended to advocate for a "self-determined" education system. From the perspective of a psychologist who is committed to the healing of the collective "Black mind," I believe that clear concepts are needed to guide our approach to education. I believe that those concepts should be communicated effectively and in a reasonably simple way so that people who are engaged in trying to educate themselves and their children will have some guidelines and criteria for recognizing "true" education when they see it. The content of such education has been frequently discussed and well researched. The special task of this book is to help us understand why people should be responsible for their own education and what they should try to accomplish in this process of developing "knowledge of self." As we enter this new millenium, we must be clear that our positions must be dictated by our empowerment as human beings. We cannot continue to be reactors or participants in the vision and worldview of people who see us as fixtures in their world rather than as co-builders of a world that places our priorities and perspective at the top of the human agenda. The experiences of human degradation and challenge that have been endured and overcome by people of color during the last half of this millenium have been preparatory for African people. It has given properly educated African people a perspective on moral, social and spiritual world leadership that must be included in the continued progress of human beings on this planet. To exclude the perceptions from this misrepresented and ignored perspective simply dooms the world, as we know it to a pit of its own karmic destruction. It is for this reason that there is urgency for African people in particular to "know thyself," and for all of humanity to be committed to the honest knowledge of themselves and of others.

Bibliography

Akbar, N. (1984). **From Miseducation to Education.** Jersey city, NJ: New Mind Productions.

Akbar, N. (1994). **Light from Ancient Africa.** Tallahassee, FL: Mind Productions and Assoc.

Akbar, N. (1995). **Natural Psychology and Human Transformation.** Tallahassee, FL: Mind Productions and Assoc.

Asante, M. (1980). **Afrocentricity: The Theory of Social Change.** Buffalo: Amulefi Pub. Co.

Asante, M. (1991). **The Book of African Names.** Trenton, NJ: Africa World Press.

Banks, W.C. (1982). "Deconstruction falsification: Foundations of a critical method in Black Psychology" in Enrico Jones and Sheldon Korchin (Eds.) **Minority Mental Health.** New York: Praeger Press.

Ben Jochannan, Y.(1971). **Africa Mother of Civilization.** New York: Alkebu-lan Books Associates.

Clark, C.(1972). "Black studies or the study of Black people" in R.Jones (Ed.) **Black Psychology (1st ed.)** New York: Harper & Row Pub.

Clarke, J.H.(1993). **African People in World History.** Baltimore: Black Classics Press.

Diop, C.A. (1974). **The African Origins of Civilization: Myth or Reality.** Westport. CT: Lawrence Hill & Co.

Hilliard, A.(1997). **SBA: The Reawakening of the African Mind.** Gainesville, FL: Makare Publishing Co.

Hilliard, A., Williams, L. and Damali, N. (Ed.) (1987). **The Teachings of Ptahhotep: The Oldest Book in the World.** Atlanta: Blackwood Press.

Jackson, J. G. (1970). **Introduction to African Civilization.** Secaucus, NJ: Citadel Press.

71

James, G.G.M.(1976). **Stolen Legacy.** San Francisco: Julian Richardson Associates.

Karenga, M. (1984). **Selections from the Husia (Sacred Wisdom of Ancient Egypt.)** Los Angeles: Kawaida Publications.

Leslau, C. & W.(1982). **African Proverbs.** New York: Peter Pauper Press.

Muhammad, E.(1965). **Message to the Black Man in America.** Chicago: Muhammad Mosque #2.

Nobles, W.W.(1986). **African Psychology: Towards it Reclamation, Reascension and Revitalization.** Oakland, CA: Black Family Institute Publications.

Rogers, J.A.(1961). **Africa's Gift to America.** New York: Helga M. Rogers.

Van Sertima, I.(1976). **They Came Before Columbus.** New York: Random House.

Williams, C. (1974). **The Destruction of Black Civilization.** Chicago: Third World Press.

Woodson, C.G. (1933/1990). **The Miseducation of the Negro.** Trenton, NJ: Africa World Press.

ENDNOTES

1 Woodson, Carter G.(1933/1990) The Miseducation of the Negro. Trenton, NJ: Africa World Press.
2 Akbar, Na'im (1984) From Miseducation to Education. Jersey City: New Mind Productions.
3 Ibid., ii.
4 Ibid., ii.
5 Many African-Americans have developed practices of changing their names which came out of slavery and adopting African based or other self-selected names. The tradition of the Nation of Islam under the direction of the Honorable Elijah Muhammad required the adoption of the letter "X" for a last name in order to negate the slave name. "Malcolm X" was one of the most famous users of this pattern. In the appendix there is a name change ritual which will assist people who are interested in formally changing their names through a re-naming ceremony.
6 Ibid., xii-xiii.
7 Ibid., 84.
8 Ibid., 2-3; 6.
9 Muhammad, E. (1965) Message to the Black Man in America. Chicago, IL: Muhammad Mosque #2, p.31.
10 Akbar, N. (1994) Light From Ancient Africa. Tallahassee, FL: Mind Productions & Assoc.

[11] Akbar, N. (1995) Natural Psychology and Human Transformation. Tallahassee, FL: Mind Productions & Assoc.

[12] Ibid.

[13] Karenga, M. (1984) Selections from the Husia (Sacred Wisdom of Ancient Egypt). Los Angeles: Kawaida Publications.

[14] Hilliard, A., Williams, L. & Damali , N. Eds. (1987) The Teachings of Ptahhotep: The Oldest Book in the World. Atlanta: Blackwood Press.

[15] Ibid., 20.

[16] Ibid., 51.

[17] Leslau, Charlotte & Wolf (1982). African Proverbs. New York: Peter Pauper Press, pp.42,45,25,30 &31.

[18] Ibid., 55.

[19] Leslau. Ibid., 16.

[20] Ibid.,56-57.

[21] Ibid., 56.

[22] Ibid., xiii.

[23] Ibid., 32.

[24] Ibid., 32.

[25] Ibid.

[26] Holy Qur'an, 2:256.

[27] Banks, W.C.(1982) Deconstruction falsification: Foundations of a critical method in Black Psychology in Enrico Jones and Sheldon Korchin (Eds.) Minority Mental Health. New York: Praeger Press.

[28] Ibid., 39.

[29] Van Sertima, Ivan (1976). They Came Before Columbus. New York: Random House.

[30] Diop, Cheikh Anta (1974). The African Origin of Civilization: Myth or Reality. Westport, CT: Lawrence Hill & Co.

[31] Nobles, Wade W. (1986). African Psychology: Towards its Reclamation, Reascension and Revitalization. Oakland, CA: Black Family Institute Publication (p. 83).

[32] Clark, Cedric (1972) "Black Studies or the Study of Black People," in R. Jones (Ed.) Black Psychology. New York: Harper and Row Pub. (p. 5).

[33] Adopted by this writer from a translation of "Libation Oratory" by Marion Kilson (1968/1969). "The Ga Naming Rite," in Anthropos, 63/64, pp.904-920.

APPENDIX

A Ritual for Re-Naming '

PROCESSIONAL: The Drummers should engage in a festive drumbeat to announce the opening of the ceremony and the beginning of the procession. The procession is led by (1) the *Officiating Elder* followed by (2) the *Libator* and (3) the *Initiate(s)* flanked by (same gender as Initiate) blood relatives. (This may be as many as four relatives on all sides or a minimum of two with one before and one behind.) The ritual party should enter into the ritual area at a slow rate with the drums continuing to beat. The procession may be as elaborate or as simple as you choose. It can proceed through the community or simply from another room in the house.

        Officiating Elder: *This will be the master of ceremonies for the ritual and will lead the party through the various aspects of the ritual. This should be a respected Elder of the Community who may or may not be a member of the Initiates family.*

        Libator: *This will be a person familiar with the ceremony and procedure for the pouring of Libation which is a form of prayer and remembrance of the Creator and His agents, The Ancestors.*

        Initiate: *This is the person or persons who have chosen to select a new name and be re-named.*

The opening Libation Oratory[33] (This is led by the Elder or Libator after the procession has assembled in the meeting area for the ceremony.)

Hail! Hail! Hail! May happiness come!   *(Response of all: "Ashaa!)*
Hail, may happiness come!   *(Ashaa!)*
Whenever we join up to make a circle, may
       Our chain be complete.   *(Ashaa!)*
Whenever we dig a well, may we come
       Upon water.   *(Ashaa!)*
May it be darkness behind the stranger who
       Has come.   *(Ashaa!)*
And brightness before him.   *(Ashaa!)*
May we leave whole, and
       May we return in whole.   *(Ashaa!)*

May his/her mother have long life.   *(Ashaa!)*

May his/her father have long life.   *(Ashaa!)*

May s/he eat by the labor of his/her five fingers.   *(Ashaa!)*
May s/he labor for his/her father.   *(Ashaa!)*
May s/he labor for his/her mother.   *(Ashaa!)*

May we forgive him/her everything forgivable.   *(Ashaa!)*
May s/he grow to respect the world.   *(Ashaa!)*
May s/he not steal.   *(Ashaa!)*
May s/he not lie.   *(Ashaa!)*
May s/he be blessed.   *(Ashaa!)*
May s/he prosper.   *(Ashaa!)*

May his/her path be straightened for him/her.   *(Ashaa!)*
May all mishaps be cleared away.   *(Ashaa!)*
Life and prosperity to all his/her children
       And those yet unborn.   *(Ashaa!)*

Hail may happiness come!   *(Ashaa! Ashaa!)*

---

᠔ Appreciation is extended to Professor Abu Shardow Abarry of the Department of African-American Studies at Temple University for his helpful suggestions in designing this ceremony.

The Pouring of Libation for the Ancestors: (Performed by the Libator.)

The forms of these ceremonies vary widely, but they are intended to acknowledge the contributions and continued spiritual presence of our ancestors. The person identified as the Libator should already be familiar with this ceremony and should be prepared to explain what is being done to those present who may not understand the ritual. The Libator may also perform an appropriate prayer following the performance of the Libation.

Reading from the Inspired Word (Holy Qur'an, Holy Bible, Husia or other appropriate scripture):

Either the Libator, the Elder or some other appropriate person should select an appropriate selection from Divine Revelation that speaks to the importance of a name.

The Occasion:

A knowledgeable Elder should present instructions about the significance of this ceremony. The Elder should explain why a person named in the tradition of former slaves might consider changing their name to a name more consistent with their true culture and tradition. It is important to note that the change of name intends no disrespect for those immediate ancestors and parents who have passed on the slavery name, but the change represents the reestablishment of the true identity of a person who has been lost from the true knowledge of themselves.

The Altar:

For use in the ritual, there should be a fireproof bowl or other surface in which some items can be burned later in the ceremony. There should also be a flowerpot of dirt for the symbolic burial of theses ashes. It would be good to have either pictures or other personal items from the ancestors of the initiate on the altar as well. Carvings, cloth or other items connected with Africa should also be on the altar. The initiate should select some objects of significance to him/her that they would like to include on the altar. At this point, either the initiate, a family member or another selected person should talk about the altar or why the objects that are included (Explanations for the urn and flowerpot can be saved until these items are used in the ritual).

Burial of the Slave's name:

The Elder calls forth a parent (preferably father) or other member of the initiate's family. The **Elder** says: *What name was this man (woman) given at birth?*

The **Family Member** replies: *(S)he was given the Christian slave name of* _____ (state the first and middle given names of the initiate.)
Elder: *Have you brought dignity to the European slave name* _____ *that you were given?*

Initiate: *I have brought dignity to the European slave name* _____ *that I was given at birth.*

Elder: *You may now destroy the foreign name that was given to you at birth.*

The relative who provided the name above should now give the initiate his/her first and middle names written on a piece of paper. The Initiate turns to the left in a counter clockwise direction, four (4) steps making a complete circle. The four (4) steps in the turn represent the four (4) centuries that the correct name has been taken away. As the **Initiate** turns (s)he states at each step of the turn: *I now return the foreigner's name* _____ *that was given to me at birth.*

The Initiate then gives the piece of paper on which the name is written to the Elder. The Elder burns the paper in the urn on the altar.

Elder: *What is the family name that this man (woman) was born into?* The same or another family member should say: *His/her family was given the name of their slave master that was* _____.

The same procedure that was done for the given names is now repeated for the family name except the **Elder** says: *Have you and your family brought dignity to this name that was given to you?*

Initiate: *My family and I have brought dignity to the slave master's name that we were given.*

Elder: *You may now destroy the slave name that was given to your family during their captivity.*

While making his four (4)step circle as above the **Initiate** says: *I destroy the name that was given to my family during our captivity.*

The Elder should burn the family name as was done for the given names. The initiate should bury all of the ashes in the dirt on the altar after the family name has been burned. The dirt containing the ashes should later be returned to the earth outside.

Elder: *We humbly pay homage to our ancestors who labored under these alien names. We thank them for their sacrifices and we ask them to join us in blessing this occasion. We seek not to dissociate ourselves from them and their sacrifices, but from the oppression that made their suffering necessary. We celebrate them and their fine work and we ask the Creator to grant them continued blessings. We ask their blessings and support in the burial of a painful past. We celebrate the dignity that they brought to the names that were put on them by cruel masters who sought to take them from themselves.*

THE RE-NAMING:

The **Elder:** (The initiate should be seated in front of the Elder and the Elder should state.) *You shall be called Kwesi. (of course, the name in this blank should be the first given name which is to be given to the initiate. The name should be pronounced followed by a thorough description of the meaning of this name.) The name Kwesi is common among the Akan people of Ghana and it refers to one born on Sunday for the Asante people. This same name among the GA people of Ghana means Conquering Strength. This name refers to the power of the inner will. Though it is a warrior's name, it does not refer to the power of domination, but to the power of the will. It describes the power to conquer the enemies within oneself and to overcome the challenges of life. The person who carried this name acknowledges that he also carries the power to overcome whatever obstacles may be put in his path either by circumstance or by distractions within himself. Victory always comes to Kwesi because he is endowed with the ability for inner self-mastery that gives him the power to overcome difficulties with compassion and concern. You are, with this name, never able to claim weakness as an excuse. You are a natural conqueror, but you conquer enemies and difficulties with compassion and concern. You are also gifted to conquer people and situations. This is a power that can be used for proper advancement or for exploitation. If you use it for exploitation the very strength will become your weakness. You will find yourself shackled and pursued by those things that were conquered out of greed and selfishness. We ask that the Creator who is the Giver and Source of all strength will grant you the power to master this* *great gift. We ask that this "Conquering Strength" should be used to advance our people and advance you and our collective humanity.*

Do you fully understand the meaning of this name and the responsibility that you are assuming in taking this name?

Initiate: *Yes, Elder, I do understand.*

Elder: (To the Initiate:) *Repeat after me. You are (I am) Kwesi.* Initiate repeats the name three times with echo from the community as he turns slowly in a circle to the right. **The Elder** says *You Are* _____. The **Initiate** says *I am* _____. The Drummers beat with each turn while the community echoes back *You Are* _____.

The same procedure is done for each of the names to be taken. **The Elder** should preface the definition of the last or family name by saying: *You and your seed throughout all time shall be called* _____.

Initiate's Pledge: When the last name has been given, the **Elder** leads the following pledge that is repeated in phrases by the **Initiate:**

I, who was at birth named _____ *(the full birth name that has been given up) do affirm in the presence of these witnesses and the spiritual and ancestral visitors who have joined us, my desire to reclaim a name of my great African Ancestors. I have chosen to make this change of my own free will. I recognize that in centuries past, my family who preceded me was forbidden to use their true spiritual and ancestral names. They were forced to wear the foreign and alien names of their conquerors. I wish to be known from this day forward as* _____ _____ *and I wish myself and my future offspring to be known by the family name* _____.

Elder: *You are now* _____ *(full adopted name). From this day forward you are to be known by all people as:* _____. *In taking this name you have chosen to break the chains of our slavery and to spiritually reconnect your self and your family to the lost link with our Ancient Ancestors back to the beginning of time. For you and your seed, you have officially ended slavery today. We close the door on the kidnapping that robbed you from yourself. You have been restored to your Ancestors and have corrected the wrong done to those generations that were* *forced to live and die with an alien name. Those ancient and recently kidnapped ancestors are here today and cheer you as the one who has reconnected the circle. You have taken on a great responsibility. You have freed yourself, but you have pledged to live up to those outstanding attributes that you now carry in your name.*

(The Elder then makes appropriate comments about the meaning of the entire name and its significance for the community and the responsibility of the initiate to live up to the demands of that name.)

Shemhotep (or peace be with you) _____ _____

_____,

The Initiate Speaks: The Initiate shares with the community the significance that his/her new name means to him/her. They should also indicate the commitment that they are making to the name, to the ancestors and to the community in taking this name.

The Closing: Each member of the community, beginning with the Initiate's immediate family greets and embraces the Initiate repeating the benediction: *Shemhotep* _____ _____ _____, *may the Creator bless you and your seed forever.* This greeting is accompanied by Drumming.

Closing Meditation and Reading by Elder or other person.

A community-wide feast of celebration follows the Ritual of Re-naming.

OTHER PUBLICATIONS BY DR. NA'IM AKBAR

BREAKING THE CHAINS OF PSYCHOLOGICAL SLAVERY

THE COMMUNITY OF SELF

LIGHT FROM ANCIENT AFRICA

NATURAL PSYCHOLOGY AND HUMAN TRANSFORMATION

VISIONS FOR BLACK MEN

AUDIO AND VIDEO CASSETTES OF DR. AKBAR'S LECTURES ARE ALSO AVAILABLE FROM:

MIND PRODUCTIONS & ASSOCIATES, INC.
P.O. BOX 11221
TALLAHASSEE, FL 32302
(850) 222-1764

WEB PAGE ADDRESS: HTTP//WWW.MINDPRO.COM
E-MAIL ADDRESS: MINDPRO@MINDPRO.COM